OUTSTANDING DISSERTATIONS IN LINGUISTICS

Edited by

Laurence Horn
Yale University

T0384830

A ROUTLEDGE SERIES

Outstanding Dissertations in Linguistics

Laurence Horn, *General Editor*

THE UPS AND DOWNS OF CHILD LANGUAGE

Experimental Studies on Children's Knowledge of Entailment Relationships and Polarity Phenomena

Andrea Gualmini

ROUTLEDGE
New York & London

Published in 2005 by
Routledge
Taylor & Francis Group
711 Third Avenue
New York, NY 10017
www.routledge-ny.com

First issued in paperback 2011

Library of Congress Cataloging-in-Publication Data
    Gualmini, Andrea, 1971-
      The ups and downs of child language : experimental studies in children's knowledge of
    entailment relationships and polarity phenomena / Andrea Gualmini.
         p. cm. — (Outstanding dissertations in linguistics)
      Includes bibliographical references and index.
      ISBN 0-415-97125-X
       1. Language acquisition. 2. Language awareness in children. I. Title. II. Series.

    P118.G827 2004
    401'.93—dc22   2004051430

ISBN13: 978-0-415-97125-6 (hbk)
ISBN13: 978-0-415-51294-7 (pbk)

Table of Contents

Acknowledgments

I would like to express my gratitude to my advisor Stephen Crain. I started working with Stephen since my first days at the University of Maryland at College Park and I am not willing to stop! Much of what I learned from Stephen will be evident upon reading the dissertation. Of course, there's Continuity and all that. There is something that might not transpire from reading the dissertation, however. That is the way Stephen guided me throughout my graduate studies. After I gave the committee members a copy of the dissertation, I was struck by how easy it all seemed to be. I owe this to Stephen, who led me through all the right steps and never let me feel the burden of what would come next. Stephen has provided me with a model that I will always look up to in my own career.

Norbert Hornstein was the first person I met when I arrived at the University of Maryland. After five minutes with Norbert, I could tell I was in for a big change. I only wish it happened earlier. I have always looked forward to my meetings with Norbert, and I have always been impressed by how quickly he could see where I was going. I would like to thank Norbert for being so helpful and supportive throughout my entire graduate career.

I am also grateful for the opportunity to discuss my work with Paul Pietroski. Paul has always provided valuable suggestions concerning the details of my work, as well as the general direction of my research. He deserves special thanks for being so supportive of all aspects of my research project.

The next person I would like to thank is Rozz Thornton. Rozz has been extremely helpful since my first days at Maryland. I am grateful for the time she spent with me at Center for Young Children always looking over my shoulder as I was learning how to conduct experiments. I would also like to thank Rozz for numerous comments on the dissertation draft.

I would also like to thank John Horty for agreeing to serve on the dissertation committee as the Dean's Representative.

In addition to the committee members, I had the privilege of discussing some of my work with many people who were unlucky enough to be within reach. First, I would like to thank Julien Musolino for important and helpful discussions. Julien and I only overlapped for a few days at the University of Maryland in 1998. Initially, the overlap between our research interests was small. More recently, however, the overlap has become bigger and bigger. Eventually, we realized that we had to deal with it and write a paper together. And, since I can say pretty much all I want here, what a paper we wrote! I would also like to thank Martin Hackl, who was very helpful during his two years at the University of Maryland. I learned a lot from random conversations with Martin, and I really wished he was still at Maryland during the last stages of this dissertation. Finally, I would like to thank all the faculty, students, and visitors of the Department of Linguistics at the University of Maryland with whom I had the pleasure to work over the last five years. I would like to single out Scott Fults, Howard Lasnik, Juan Uriagereka and Amy Weinberg for discussing with me different parts of the dissertation.

Furthermore, I gained valuable feedback from audiences at the Boston University Conference on Language Development (2001, 2002) the Linguistic Society of America (2001, 2002, 2003), NELS (2002), Sinn und Bedeutung (2002), MIT (Department of Linguistics and Philosophy) and Indiana University (Department of Speech and Hearing Science). In particular, I thank Danny Fox, Irene Heim, Jeff Lidz, Anna Papafragou, Anna Szabolcsi and Ken Wexler for discussion of the research documented in this dissertation.

My graduate studies at the University of Maryland have been supported by the Linguistics Department through various Graduate Assistantships. My fifth year at Maryland was partially supported by a Dissertation Fellowship awarded by the Graduate School. I gratefully acknowledge these sources for providing me peace of mind. I am also grateful to the organizers of the Boston University Conference on Language Development for the Paula Menyuk Travel award that allowed me to attend the conference in 2002.

Before I started my graduate studies, I studied linguistics with Gennaro Chierchia and Maria Teresa Guasti. Gennaro and Teresa also helped me with my desire to pursue graduate studies in the US and I would like to thank them for their support.

I also thank all the faculty of the Department of Linguistics at MIT, who gave me the opportunity to write the dissertation without having to worry (too much) about what would come next.

During the past five years, I spent more time working on the premises of a pre-school than in university classrooms. All the experiments reported in this dissertation were conducted at the Center for Young Children (CYC) at the University of Maryland. I thank the children, teachers, and staff of that school for making this experience so enjoyable. In particular, I would like to thank Fran Favaretto and Anne Daniel for their invaluable support.

Over the last few years I have come to appreciate the many virtues of the Truth Value Judgment task. Among other things, I have come to appreciate the fact that it takes two people to conduct an experiment. This feature of the experimental design gave me the opportunity to spend many hours with Shani Abada, Jessica Ehrlich, Andrea Frost, Amanda Gardner, Lia Gravelle, Megan Gilliver, Lindsay Iadevaia, Ruth Lopes, Simona Maciukaite, Utako Minai, Beth Rabbin, Eileen Rivers, Nadia Shihab, Yi-Ching Su and Andrea Zukowski. I am grateful to all of them for their help in conducting the experiments and for being so generous with their time.

Next come some of the people who made life more enjoyable during the last five years. Among all my friends, I thank my Sunday soccer fellows for being so considerate of me when I told them I had no health insurance. I thank Massimo and Tiziana who always made me feel at home. Auri, Gianluca and Marco deserve many thanks for not letting our friendship change.

The decision to move to the US affected many people. Among all the people who supported me, I would like to thank Adriano for his encouragement and Ambrogio and Elia for their understanding.

My parents deserve many thanks for teaching me the value of education. I thank them for their encouragement and support through all these years.

Finally, I thank Luisa who helped me with the conception of the research project, the execution of the experiments, the discussion of the experimental findings and the editing of the dissertation. And this was only the least important part of what she's done for me.

This dissertation is dedicated to my zio Carlo.

THE UPS AND DOWNS OF CHILD LANGUAGE

OUTSTANDING DISSERTATIONS IN LINGUISTICS

Introduction

Entailment relations among sentences are relevant for several distributional and interpretive phenomena across natural languages. From the perspective of the acquisitionist, entailment relations provide an interesting case study in that a fairly complex theoretical apparatus is needed to account for seemingly simple facts. Consider the following pair of questions.

(1)   a.   Would you like something to drink?
           b.   Would you like anything to drink?

Both questions in (1) are grammatical. Furthermore, they are quite similar in meaning. These similarities disappear once we consider some possible answers to the questions in (1).

(2)   a.   Yes, please. I would love something to drink!
           b.   *Yes, please. I would love anything to drink!

(3)   a.   *No, thank you. I do not want something!
           b.   No, thank you. I do not want anything!

Over the last thirty years, several phenomena have been discussed in conjunction with the facts summarized above. These include the logically valid inferences that are licensed by various linguistic expressions as well as the interpretation of sentences containing logical operators such as the disjunction *or*. As a result of this research enterprise, different properties have been held responsible for the observed facts. As a side effect, linguistic research has also uncovered several interesting quirks that arise because of the particular way natural languages make reference to entailment relations. In the present study, we investigate these quirks from the perspective of children acquiring their first language.

The dissertation is organized as follows. Chapter 1 introduces the relevant linguistic phenomena as well as three alternative models of language acquisition. We consider the acquisition scenarios predicted by these models for the phenomena introduced in that chapter.

Chapter 2 provides a review of previous research on children's knowledge of entailment relations and polarity phenomena. In addition, we present an experimental investigation that addresses some questions that are left unanswered by previous research.

In Chapter 3, we turn to a core feature of grammatical competence, namely the structure dependence of grammatical operations. We use children's knowledge of polarity phenomena as a case study of structure dependence in child language.

In Chapter 4, we put aside some of the broader issues from earlier chapters, and turn to children's understanding of quantification. In particular, we focus on children's understanding of the universal quantifier *every*, one of the most investigated topic by contemporary research in child language. In that chapter, children's knowledge of polarity phenomena is used as a benchmark for evaluating previous accounts of children's understanding of the universal quantifier.

Children's interpretation of quantifiers in negative sentences is the topic of Chapter 5. We will start with the conflicting findings documented by previous research on positive and negative polarity phenomena in child language. We review some proposals presented in the literature which claim that children differ from adults in the way negative sentences are interpreted, and we investigate whether or not the observed differences call for a grammatical explanation.

Finally, we bring together the phenomena investigated in Chapters 4 and 5, by considering children's interpretation of sentences containing multiple scope-bearing elements. This is the topic of Chapter 6, where we investigate children's interpretation of sentences containing three scope bearing elements: *every*, *not* and *some*.

CHAPTER 1

Language and Acquisition

Much contemporary research on child language is guided by the poverty of the stimulus argument. This argument is for the most part based on two observations. First, young children possess a rich linguistic competence. Second, the input to which young children are exposed undermines their linguistic competence in many respects. To reconcile the mismatch between the rich linguistic competence shown by children and the impoverished input to which they are exposed, it is inferred that innate linguistic knowledge assists the child in the process of language acquisition. The role of innate linguistic principles is to restrict the child's hypothesis space, so that the child can make the most out of the impoverished input (see Chomsky, 1980a).

In recent years, the basic premises of the poverty of the stimulus argument have been challenged. Some researchers have denied that young children possess adult linguistic competence (see Tomasello, 2000). Other researchers have denied that the input to which children are exposed is seriously impoverished (see Pullum and Scholz, 2002). In this chapter, we consider both (kinds of) challenges to the poverty of the stimulus argument. We also examine one line of research that arguably constitutes the strongest nativist position within the generative framework. This is the Continuity Assumption, which proposes that child language is constrained by the boundaries of Universal Grammar (UG) throughout the entire course of language development.

The three models of language acquisition that we discuss will be evaluated throughout the present dissertation. In conducting this evaluation, we will consider one semantic property, which underpins various phenomena of natural languages. This property has to do with entailment relations between different sentences. The relevance of entailment relations for natural languages takes on different forms. Entailment relations regulate the use of particular expressions that show a limited distribution, e.g., so called negative and positive polarity items. Moreover, entailment relations play a role in more subtle phenomena, namely the interpretation of expressions like the disjunction operator *or* and a subclass of positive polarity items. The relevant facts will be introduced in the next section. We will argue that this cluster of phenomena provides a useful yardstick for evaluating the alternative models of language acquisition which are the focus of current debate.

1.1 Entailment Relations, Polarity Items and Inferences across Natural Languages

This section introduces the linguistic phenomena that will be considered throughout the present study. For expository purposes, we start by considering the following pair of questions.

(1)   a.   Would you like <u>something</u> to drink?
       b.   Would you like <u>anything</u> to drink?[1]

Both questions in (1) are grammatical. Furthermore, they are quite similar in meaning. Let us now consider the possible answers to the questions in (1).

(2)   a.   Yes, please. I would love <u>something</u> to drink!
       b.   *Yes, please. I would love <u>anything</u> to drink!

(3)   a.   *No, thank you. I don't want <u>something</u>![2]
       b.   No, thank you. I don't want <u>anything</u>!

The question is why a contrast is witnessed in (2) and (3), but not in (1). This puzzle has received considerable attention, beginning with Klima (1964). Over the last thirty years, several phenomena have been discussed in conjunction with the facts summarized above. As a result of this research, different properties have been held responsible for those facts. One property plays a prominent role in most accounts, however. This property is downward entailment.

---

1 We adopt the convention of underlying the expressions that provide the relevant contrast.

2 Throughout the dissertation, ungrammatical sentences will be marked with an asterisk.

1.1.1 Entailment Relations across Natural Languages

Downward entailment is a semantic property common to a variety of linguistic expressions. The defining property of downward entailing expressions is the licensing of inferences from a set to its subsets. Consider the examples in (4). Adult speakers of English recognize the inferences in (4) as valid. In each example, the difference between the two sentences is that a noun phrase, e.g., *paper*, is replaced by a second noun phrase, e.g., *good paper*, which picks out a subset of the set denoted by the first.

(4)   a.   John has not written a <u>paper</u> yet
             ⇒   John has not written a <u>good paper</u> yet.
    b.   None of the students has written a <u>paper</u> yet
             ⇒   None of the students has written a <u>good paper</u> yet.
    c.   None of the students who wrote a <u>paper</u> has received a grade yet
             ⇒   None of the students who wrote a <u>good paper</u> has received a grade yet.
    d.   John graduated without writing a <u>paper</u>
             ⇒   John graduated without writing a <u>good paper</u>.

As the invalid inferences in (5) suggest, it is easy to identify linguistic contexts that do *not* license valid inferences from a set to its subsets.[3]

(5)   a.   John wrote a <u>paper</u>
             *⇒   John wrote a <u>good paper</u>.[4]
    b.   Some of the students wrote a <u>paper</u>
             *⇒   Some of the students wrote a <u>good paper</u>.

---

3 Throughout the dissertation, we restrict our attention to expressions that generate inferences from a set to its subsets or from a set to its supersets. Thus, we will ignore all non-monotonic expressions, e.g. *exactly one, more than two and less than ten* etc.

4 We will use the symbols '*⇒' and '*⇔' to indicate invalid inferences and invalid equivalences respectively.

      c.   Some of the students who wrote a <u>paper</u> received a grade
                  *⇒   Some of the students who wrote a <u>good paper</u> received a grade.
      d.   John graduated with a <u>paper</u>
                  *⇒   John graduated with a <u>good paper</u>.[5]

It is worth pointing out the existence of linguistic expressions which, though closely related in meaning, license different inferences (i.e., they differ in the direction of entailment relations). One clear contrast of this sort arises with the prepositions *without* versus *with,* as shown in (6).

(6)   a.   John passed the class <u>without a grade</u>
                  ⇒   John passed the class <u>without a good grade</u>.
      b.   John passed the class <u>with a grade</u>
                  *⇒   John passed the class <u>with a good grade</u>.

The temporal subordinate conjunctions *before* and *after* exhibit the same contrast, as shown in (7).

(7)   a.   John graduated <u>before he wrote his first paper</u>
                  ⇒   John graduated <u>before he wrote his first good paper</u>.
      b.   John graduated <u>after he wrote his first paper</u>
                  *⇒   John graduated <u>after he wrote his first good paper</u>.

In addition to presenting a minimal pair, the contrast in (7) is interesting for a second reason. Many of the downward entailing contexts illustrated in (4) seem to have a negative component which the non-downward entailing contexts in (5) lack. In the case of (7)a, however, this is not the case. Neither sentence in (7) has a negative flavor, but the two sentences generate different entailments. Similarly, a contrast that does not involve a negative component is witnessed in (8).

---

5 Some of the examples in (4) and (5) use different tenses. Such differences are motivated by the fact that some speakers of English have a preference for the use of the present perfect tense when an adverb like *yet* is present.

(8)   a.   Every student who wrote a <u>paper</u> received a grade
                    ⇒   Every student who wrote a <u>good paper</u>
                             received a grade.
       b.   Every student wrote a <u>paper</u>
                    *⇒   Every student wrote a <u>good paper</u>.

The contrast in (8) allows us to comment on another feature of downward entailment. Downward entailment is not a property of a sentence as a whole. Rather, downward entailment is limited to a specific environment. As (8)a shows, the universal quantifier *every* is downward entailing on the subject noun phrase. However, as witnessed by (8)b, the universal quantifier *every* does not create a downward entailing environment for the object noun phrase.

1.1.2 Polarity Items and Entailment Relations

Thus far, the property of downward entailment seems to have limited consequences for natural languages. Downward entailment only describes the environments in which a noun phrase can be substituted with one that picks out a subset of the denotation of the original noun phrase without affecting the truth of the original sentence. The relevance of entailment relations for natural languages becomes more tangible if we turn to the distribution of negative polarity items (NPIs), e.g., the words *any* and *ever* in English. As shown by the grammaticality of the sentences in (9) and (10), these negative polarity items are permitted in the same linguistic environments that license inferences from sets to their subsets (e.g., the linguistic environments in (4)).

(9)   a.   John didn't write <u>any</u> paper.
       b.   None of the students wrote <u>any</u> paper.
       c.   None of the students who wrote <u>any</u> paper received a grade.
       d.   John graduated without <u>any</u> paper.

(10)   a.   John didn't <u>ever</u> write a paper.[6]
       b.   None of the students <u>ever</u> wrote a paper.
       c.   None of the students who <u>ever</u> wrote a paper received a grade.
       d.   John graduated without <u>ever</u> writing a paper.

---

6 For some speakers, the adverb *never* should be used in (10)a (see Hoecksema, 1999).

Moreover, linguistic environments that fail to license inferences from sets to their subsets (i.e., the linguistic environments in (5)), also ban negative polarity items, as shown by the ungrammaticality of the sentences in (11) and (12).

(11)   a.   *John wrote <u>any</u> paper.
        b.   *Some student wrote <u>any</u> paper.
        c.   *Some student who wrote <u>any</u> paper received a grade.
        d.   *John graduated with <u>any</u> paper.

(12)   a.   *John <u>ever</u> wrote a paper.
        b.   *Some student <u>ever</u> wrote a paper.
        c.   *Some student who <u>ever</u> wrote a paper received a grade.

Still further parallels can be drawn between downward entailment and the distribution of negative polarity items. Examples (13) and (14) indicate that negative polarity items are tolerated with the preposition *without*, but not *with*, and with the temporal conjunction *before*, but not *after*.

(13)   a.   John passed the class <u>without</u> any grade.
        b.   *John passed the class <u>with</u> any grade.

(14)   a.   John graduated <u>before</u> he wrote any paper.
        b.   *John graduated <u>after</u> he wrote any paper.

Furthermore, the contrast between environments which license negative polarity items and environments which do not license these items cannot be assimilated to the contrast between negative-like and affirmative-like environments (see (14), (15) and (16)).

(15)   a.   Every student who <u>ever</u> wrote a paper received a grade.
        b.   *Every student <u>ever</u> wrote a paper.

(16)   a.   Every student who wrote <u>any</u> paper received a grade.
        b.   *Every student wrote <u>any</u> paper.

In recent years, research on polarity items has attempted to specify the inventory of expressions whose appearance is limited to downward entailing environments. This research has also uncovered numerous expressions that *resist* downward entailing environments, however. Roughly speaking, these positive polarity items show the opposite behavior of negative polarity items. The behavior of some of these positive polarity items, as discussed by Baker (1970), is illustrated below.

(17)   a.   *John didn't <u>already</u> write a paper.
         b.   *John wouldn't <u>rather</u> write a paper.
         c.   *John couldn't <u>just as well</u> write a paper.
         d.   *John doesn't <u>still</u> write papers.
         e.   *John doesn't <u>somewhat</u> like writing papers.[7]

(18)   a.   John <u>already</u> wrote a paper.
         b.   John would <u>rather</u> write a paper.
         c.   John could <u>just as well</u> write a paper.
         d.   John <u>still</u> writes papers.
         e.   John <u>somewhat</u> likes writing papers.

Classifying negative and positive polarity items has proved a much harder task than our discussion suggests. In particular, it has been shown that different negative polarity items are subject to different restrictions. For example, although words like *any* and *ever* show a different distribution from *some* and *always*, their distribution is broader than that of other negative polarity items like *yet* or *budge an inch* (see Zwarts, 1998). By illustration, consider the contrast below:

(19)   a.   No students wrote <u>any</u> paper.
         b.   No students have written a paper <u>yet</u>.

(20)   a.   At most three students wrote <u>any</u> paper.
         b.   *At most three students have written a paper <u>yet</u>.

Similarly, cross-linguistic research has uncovered the existence of positive polarity items that can only occur in a subset of upward entailing contexts (see van der Wouden, 1994). In order to make sense of these additional restrictions

---

7 Some of the examples in (17) become acceptable if they are intended as denials of the corresponding affirmative sentences. This is not the context under consideration (see Baker, 1970).

on the distribution of polarity sensitive expressions, we need to introduce a third consequence of downward entailment.

1.1.3 Entailment and Logical Inferences across Natural Languages

The third property of downward entailing operators is witnessed in the interpretation of (sentences containing) disjunction. In fact, for any downward entailing operator OP_{DE}, statements containing disjunction logically entail the corresponding statements containing conjunction according to the scheme in (21).

(21) $OP_{DE}(A \text{ or } B) \Rightarrow OP_{DE}(A) \text{ and } OP_{DE}(B)$

The scheme of inference in (21) bears a close resemblance to (one direction of) one of De Morgan's laws of propositional logic:[8]

(22) $\neg(P \vee Q) \Leftrightarrow \neg P \wedge \neg Q$

Across natural languages, the scheme in (21) extends beyond negation, however. It holds for all downward entailing operators, as the examples in (23) show.

(23)   a.   John has not written a paper <u>or</u> made a presentation yet
                       $\Rightarrow$ John has not written a paper yet <u>and</u> John has not made a presentation yet.
          b.   None of the students have written a paper <u>or</u> made a presentation yet
                       $\Rightarrow$ None of the students have written a paper yet <u>and</u> none of the students have made a presentation yet.
          c.   None of the students who have written a paper <u>or</u> made a presentation received a grade yet
                       $\Rightarrow$ None of the students who have written a paper received a grade yet <u>and</u> none of the students who have made a presentation received a grade yet.

---

8 See Partee, ter Meulen and Wall (1990).

    d.   John passed the class without a paper <u>or</u> a presentation

            ⇒   John passed the class without a paper <u>and</u> John passed the class without a presentation.

Higginbotham (1991) refers to this phenomenon as the 'conjunctive' interpretation of disjunction. We will adopt Higginbotham's terminology for convenience. However, it should be clear that, strictly speaking, the interpretation of the disjunction *or* is simply the inclusive-*or* interpretation, proposed by classical logic (see Horn, 1989). In other words, the meaning of *or* is not different in downward and upward entailing environments. Possible differences in the entailment pattern for the entire sentence originate from the *interaction* between *or* and other operators (see Crain, Gualmini and Meroni, 2000). A better, though less reader-friendly, way of capturing the scheme in (21) would be to say that sentences containing disjunction in the scope of a downward entailing operator entail the validity of the sentences in which the same operator has scope over one of the disjuncts. (i.e., $OP_{DE}(A \text{ or } B)$ entails $OP_{DE}(A)$ as well as $OP_{DE}(B)$).

    As should now be expected, upward entailing environments do not give rise to inferences of the sort in (21). As a consequence, native speakers of English do not recognize the inferences in (24) as valid.[9]

(24)   a.   John wrote a paper <u>or</u> made a presentation

            *⇒   John wrote a paper <u>and</u> John made a presentation.

      b.   Some student wrote a paper <u>or</u> made a presentation

            *⇒   Some student wrote a paper <u>and</u> some student made a presentation.

      c.   Some student who wrote a paper <u>or</u> made a presentation received a grade

            *⇒   Some student who wrote a paper received a grade <u>and</u> some student who made a presentation received a grade.

---

9 The use of the scalar term *or* in descriptions of past events is likely to trigger different implicatures, thereby leading to the infelicity of the sentences (see Grice, 1975; Horn, 1989 and Levinson, 2000). However, the inferences do not go through even if the relevant sentences are presented in contexts that typically cancel implicatures, such as predictions about events that have not taken place yet.

    d.   John passed the class with a paper <u>or</u> a presentation
                 *⇒   John passed the class with a paper <u>and</u> John passed the class with a presentation.

Upward entailing environments tend to obey the alternative inference scheme in (25), with relevant examples provided in (26).

(25)   OP(A or B) ⇒ OP(A) or OP(B) [10]

(26)   a.   John wrote a paper <u>or</u> made a presentation
                 ⇒   John wrote a paper <u>or</u> John made a presentation.
      b.   Some student wrote a paper <u>or</u> made a presentation
                 ⇒   Some student wrote a paper <u>or</u> some student made a presentation.
      c.   Some student who wrote a paper <u>or</u> made a presentation received a grade
                 ⇒   Some student who wrote a paper received a grade <u>or</u> some student who made a presentation received a grade.
      d.   John passed the class with a paper <u>or</u> a presentation
                 ⇒   John passed the class with a paper <u>or</u> John passed the class with a presentation.

Before we summarize the present discussion, let us go back to (21), reported below as (27).

(27) OP_{DE}(A or B) ⇒ OP_{DE}(A) and OP_{DE}(B)

---

10 Exceptions to the scheme in (25) are possible, however. For example, the nuclear scope of the universal quantifier *every* patterns differently, i.e., *Every student will write a paper or make a presentation* *⇒ *Every student will write a paper or every student will make a presentation*. To see that this inference is not valid, consider a context in which one student wrote a paper, one student made a presentation and one student did both. In such a context, *Every student will write a paper or make a presentation* is true, whereas both *Every student will write a paper* and *Every student will make a presentation* are false. Thus the left-hand side of the scheme in (25) is true, whereas its right-hand side is true. The relevant context will be investigated experimentally in Chapter 4.

It is important to observe that the converse of (27) does not always hold. In short, only one direction of the relevant De Morgan's law holds for all downward entailing operators. Inferences in the opposite direction are only licensed by a subset of downward entailing operators.[11] A downward entailing operator that only obeys one direction of the first De Morgan's law is *at most n Ns*.[12]

(28) a. At most three students wrote a paper or made a presentation
$\Rightarrow$ At most three students wrote a paper and at most three students made a presentation.

 b. At most three students wrote a paper or made a presentation
$*\Leftarrow$ At most three students wrote a paper and at most three students made a presentation.

We refer the reader to van der Wouden (1994) and Zwarts (1998) for a classification of negative (and positive) polarity items that is based on the observation that not all DE operators generate entailments according to the inverse of the scheme in (21). For present purposes, we can briefly observe that the different inferences licensed by downward entailing operators provide a first way of accounting for the lack of uniformity in the class of negative (and positive) polarity items (but see also Israel, 1998).[13]

We will not be concerned with the different subclasses of downward entailing environments, since we are primarily interested in properties that are common to all downward entailing environments. Thus, we would like to focus on the fact that the correlation between downward entailment and the licensing of inferences in accordance with (one direction of) one of the De Morgan's laws is not subject to the same amount of variation displayed by the distribution of negative (and positive) polarity items.

---

11 Operators that license inferences in accordance with (both directions) of the first De Morgan's law are called antiadditive.

12 Downward entailing operators can be classified further, depending on how they behave with respect to the second De Morgan's law, i.e., $\neg(P \wedge Q) \Leftrightarrow \neg P \vee \neg Q$ (see van der Wouden, 1994). Operators that generate inferences in accordance with both De Morgan's laws are called antimorphic. Negation is an example of antimorphic operator.

13 See our examples in (19) and (20).

1.1.4 Constraints on Entailments, Polarity Items and Inferences across Natural Languages

Having illustrated a variety of ways in which the semantic property of downward entailment manifests itself in natural languages, it is pertinent to consider the structural circumstances in which the relevant properties apply. A tempting hypothesis is that c-command dictates when downward entailing expressions are operative, and when they are not.[14] Example (29) shows that negation only licenses inferences from a set to its subsets when the relevant expression is in its c-command domain.

(29)   a.   The boy who majored in linguistics did not learn <u>a Romance language</u>

                 $\Rightarrow$ The boy who majored in linguistics did not learn <u>French</u>.

      b.   The boy who did not major in linguistics learned <u>a Romance language</u>

                 $^*\Rightarrow$ The boy who did not major in linguistics learned <u>French</u>.

In order to account for this contrast, one needs to make reference to a representation that encodes something other than linear precedence as the relevant notion. The trees below constitute a first step in this direction.

---

14 A c-commands B if and only if (i) the first branching node dominating A also dominates B, (ii) A does not dominate B and (iii) A is different from B (see Reinhart, 1976; Chomsky, 1981).

(30)

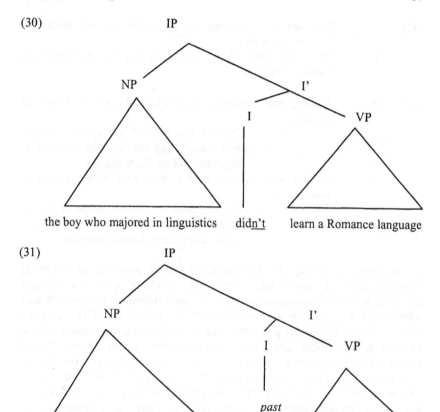

the boy who majored in linguistics   did<u>n't</u>   learn a Romance language

(31)

the boy who did<u>n't</u> major in linguistics   learn a Romance language

Thus, one could hypothesize, the relevant inference does not go through in (29)b because the c-command domain of negation does not include the VP of the main clause.

Having outlined how the structural differences between (29)a and (29)b could account for the different entailment relations, it is interesting to observe that the same contrast holds for the licensing of NPIs, as shown in (32), and for the availability of the conjunctive interpretation for the disjunction operator, as shown in (33).

(32)   a.   The boy who majored in linguistics did not learn <u>any</u> Romance language.

        b.   *The boy who did not major in linguistics learned <u>any</u> Romance language.

(33)   a.   The boy who majored in linguistics did not learn French <u>or</u> Spanish

                ⇒   The boy who majored in linguistics did not learn French <u>and</u> the boy who majored in linguistics did not learn Spanish.

        b.   The boy who did not major in linguistics learned French <u>or</u> Spanish

                *⇒   The boy who did not major in linguistics learned French <u>and</u> the boy who did not major in linguistics learned Spanish.

It is time to sum up. We have reviewed several properties of downward entailing linguistic expressions. From the point of view of semantic interpretation, these expressions are seen to license inferences from sets to their subsets, and they generate inferences in accordance with one of De Morgan's laws. From a distributional perspective, the same linguistic expressions license negative polarity items and fail to license positive polarity items. Several accounts have been proposed to explain why negative polarity items are licensed in downward entailing environments (see Ladusaw, 1979; 1980; Kadmon and Landman, 1993; Krifka, 1995; Chierchia, 2002).[15] In the present study we put aside these broader theoretical issues and we limit our attention to the descriptive generalizations pointed out in our discussion, because our concern here is with children's knowledge of downward entailment.

From an acquisition perspective, the property of downward entailment and its consequences constitute an interesting domain of research. In particular, the question of learnability assumes prominence. The question is how children achieve the intricate pattern of linguistic behavior we have summarized in this section, exclusively on the basis of positive evidence. This research question will be broached in the next section, where we also highlight some of the less transparent consequences of entailment relations across natural languages.

---

15 For important qualifications on the program inaugurated by Ladusaw (1979) see also von Fintel (1999). For alternative views see Linebarger (1980; 1987), Progovac (1988; 1994) and Israel (1998).

1.2 Quirks of Entailment

As we have seen, downward entailing operators display a complex set of distributional and interpretive properties. Consider the distribution of negative polarity items (NPIs). The occurrence of negative polarity items in adult languages is restricted to downward entailing contexts. We have even observed pairs of expressions, with related meanings (e.g., *with* and *without*, *before* and *after*), which differ in the licensing of NPIs. From an acquisition perspective, the following questions immediately arise: Is child language qualitatively different from that of adults? For example, is there a stage in language development at which children use NPIs differently from adults? A related issue involves children's knowledge of the logical properties of downward entailment. We have seen that the interpretation of sentences containing the disjunction operator *or* is sensitive to the entailment properties of the linguistic environment in which *or* occurs. Again, the question arises: Is there a stage in the course of language development at which children and adults differ in the way they interpret sentences containing the disjunction *or* in the relevant DE linguistic environment? This question was addressed in some previous studies, and a summary of the main findings of these studies will be reported in Chapter 2.

In absence of theoretical assumptions, it is difficult to spell out any predictions about the acquisition of polarity phenomena. For this reason, we will discuss the phenomena under consideration from the point of view of three alternative models of language acquisition. As we will see, these models maintain different views of what it means for children to make 'mistakes' (i.e., differ from adults). Before we turn to these three models, however, we would like to abstract away from all the linguistic accounts of polarity phenomena and highlight some further quirks of the data.

A linguistically savvy reader may be surprised by the lack of sophistication in our introduction to polarity phenomena. Taking a pre-theoretical perspective was motivated by the fact that we are ultimately concerned with child language and, as we will see momentarily, many recent accounts of child language reject the level of sophistication that linguists often presuppose. Consistent with our decision, we now recall the relevant quirks in the way natural languages make use of entailment relations, without assuming any particular theoretical framework.

The first puzzle is given by the conditions under which downward entailment is established. We have ignored most of the literature on the relation that must hold between, say, a negative polarity item and the relevant downward entailing operator. This issue has received considerable attention since the early stages of research on negative polarity items (see Hoecksema, 2000 for review). For our purposes, the relevance of this issue lies in the fact that the simplest assumption that one could make is wrong: the *presence* of a downward entailing operator in a sentence turns out to be simply irrelevant. In fact a structure dependent notion, possibly related to c-command, dictates when downward entailing operators are operative, and when they are not. Recall the examples in (29), repeated below as (34).

(34)   a.   The boy who majored in linguistics did not learn a <u>Romance language</u>
                          ⇒   The boy who majored in linguistics did not learn <u>French</u>.
          b.   The boy who did not major in linguistics learned a <u>Romance language</u>
                          *⇒   The boy who did not major in linguistics learned <u>French</u>.

The examples in (34) suggest that negation only licenses inferences from a set to its subsets when the relevant expression resides in its c-command domain. As we saw, the same contrast holds for the licensing of NPIs, and whether or not the disjunction operator receives the conjunctive interpretation.

That some structural notion is required to establish downward entailment has never surprised linguists. In fact, no linguist has ever attributed any importance to the mere *presence* of a downward entailing operator in the sentence. This does not mean that the child could not make this hypothesis, however. In fact, a domain-general learning view could maintain that this is exactly the first hypothesis a child would make. Thus, assuming that a child somehow manages to determine which operators are downward entailing, nothing prevents the child from assuming that any linguistic material following a downward entailing operator constitutes a downward entailing environment.

A second quirk of downward entailment is that it is often witnessed in negative-like environments. As we have repeatedly observed in Section 1.1, this correlation is not perfect. The lack of a perfect correlation also comes as no surprise to linguists, although early accounts (see e.g., Klima, 1964) seemed to focus on negation more than recent accounts do (see e.g., Giannakidou, 1997; 1998). Focusing on the imperfect correlation between negation and the licensing of negative polarity items would have prevented linguists from formulating any generalizations about the distribution of negative polarity items. If one only focused on negative-like contexts, for example, the contrast in the behavior of the two arguments of the universal quantifier *every* would be unexplained.[16] Relevant examples are reported below.

(35) a. Every student who wrote <u>a paper</u> received a grade
     $\Rightarrow$ Every student who wrote <u>a good paper</u> received a grade.

  b. Every student who wrote <u>any</u> paper received a grade.

  c. Every student who wrote a paper <u>or</u> made a presentation received a grade
     $\Rightarrow$ Every student who wrote a paper received a grade <u>and</u> every student who made a presentation received a grade.

(36) a. Every student wrote <u>a paper</u>
     *$\Rightarrow$ Every student wrote <u>a good paper</u>.

  b. *Every student wrote <u>any</u> paper.

  c. Every student wrote a paper <u>or</u> made a presentation
     *$\Rightarrow$ Every student wrote a paper <u>and</u> every student made a presentation.

The sentences in (35) show that the first argument of the universal quantifier *every* constitutes a downward entailing environment, despite the lack of a negative flavor. A question that immediately arises is whether children would ever make the mistake of assuming that downward entailment is restricted to negative-like environments, thereby failing to acquire knowledge of the pattern in (35).

 Considering (35) and (36) together, another aspect of the puzzle resurfaces. The contrast between (35) and (36) shows that the mere presence of a downward entailing operator does not suffice in establishing a downward entailing environment in the remainder of the sentence. In the case of *every*, a distinction has to be drawn between the subject noun phrase and the verb phrase. Thus, even if children somehow manage to acquire the pattern in (35), the question is whether they would extend the relevant generalization to the second argument of *every*, thereby failing to acquire the pattern in (36). With other linguistic

---

16 As repeatedly observed in Section 1.1, the same point is provided by the temporal conjunctions *before* and *after*.

expressions such as *no* or *some*, both arguments behave in the same way. Therefore, the child might be tempted to suppose that this is also true for the universal quantifier *every*.

The examples in (35) and (36) involve the universal quantifier *every*. This makes the contrast between (35) and (36) particularly interesting for the acquisition process. As we will see in Chapter 4, many, if not most, researchers believe that children do not have accurate understanding of this quantifier. If children do not know the semantics of *every*, however, it is difficult to see how they could grasp the contrast illustrated in (35) and (36).

Third, let us turn to a difference between negative and positive polarity items. In Section 1.1, we have highlighted the 'similarities' in behavior of these two classes of items. We have focused on an idealized generalization according to which negative polarity items can occur in the same environments in which positive polarity items cannot occur, and vice versa.[17] This is just an idealization, however, because for many so-called positive polarity items, the occurrence in a downward entailing environment does not lead to the ungrammaticality of the sentence under consideration. Rather, the occurrence of a positive polarity item often triggers some operation of the grammar that affects the interpretation of that sentence, so that the positive polarity item under consideration is not *interpreted* in a downward entailing environment. This is the case of specific indefinites containing *some*. Consider the contrast below:

(37)   a.   *John ate any pizza.
        b.   John ate some pizza.

The sentences in (37) provide us with the usual pattern: *some* can occur in an upward entailing environment, while *any* cannot. The complementary distribution between *some* and *any* breaks down, however, when we consider a downward entailing environment.

(38)   a.   John didn't eat any pizza.
        b.   John didn't eat some pizza.[18]

In (38), the occurrence of the negative polarity item *any* is acceptable, and so is the positive polarity item *some*. However, (38)b is unacceptable on the

---

17 We will illustrate a different proposal by Szabolcsi (2002a) in Chapter 6.

18 Throughout the dissertation we focus on the phonetically stressed variant of *some*.

interpretation in which *some* receives scope under negation (i.e., it is not the case that John ate some pizza). (38)b is only acceptable on the interpretation in which *some* takes scope over negation, i.e., there is some pizza that John did not eat. [19] Turning to child language, the question is whether children would distinguish between (38)a and (38)b. Both (kinds of) sentences are grammatical, thus potentially available in the input, but their interpretation is different. Making the child's task even more difficult is the fact that the difference between (38)a and (38)b lies in the application of a covert grammatical operation, possibly the only grammatical operation that does not involve any overt morphological feature (see Reinhart, 1995).

Making matter even worse for children is the observation that the contrast between the interpretation of (38)a and (38)b vanishes when both sentences are embedded in a 'negative' environment.

(39)   a.   I can't believe John didn't eat any pizza.
        b.   I can't believe John didn't eat some pizza.

Surprisingly, the sentences in (39) are quite close in meaning. Thus, the child must learn that there is a contrast between *some* and *any*, which leads to a difference in the interpretation of these items in negative sentences, as in (38). Moreover, the child must learn that this contrast is fairly subtle, as it vanishes when two negations are present.

To sum up, we have reviewed several idiosyncrasies of the way entailment relations work in natural languages.[20] Of course, the job of the linguist is to account for these idiosyncrasies. From the linguist's point of view, some of these idiosyncrasies might not be as surprising as we suggested. These idiosyncrasies could be surprising, however, for someone who cannot rely on negative evidence or experimental data. Similarly, these idiosyncrasies could be

---

19 The unavailability of the narrow scope reading of *some* seems to have become a standard assumption since Ladusaw (1979). Whether the narrow scope interpretation of *some* is unacceptable or (acceptable but) highly dispreferred, the dissimilarity between negative and positive polarity items remains: the occurrence of a positive polarity item can be rescued by a scope shifting operation while negative polarity items require the presence of a downward entailing operator at surface level (but see also Linebarger, 1987).

20 For a review of many surprising facts on the distribution of polarity sensitive items, at least from a pre-theoretic viewpoint, see van der Wouden (1994) and Israel (1998).

surprising for someone who cannot draw upon any form of syntactic structure to organize the available data. According to some models of language acquisition, this is the position in which children find themselves, in the process of acquiring their first language.

1.3 Alternative Models of Language Acquisition

In this section we consider three models of language acquisition. First, we indicate the main assumptions of these models. Then, for each model, we turn to some speculations on how it could (propose to) handle the acquisition of entailment relations and polarity phenomena. We point out which aspects of downward entailment can be used to draw specific predictions for each model.

1.3.1 The Conservative Learning Model

The first model is the Conservative Learning model, proposed by Tomasello (2000). This model rejects many of the assumptions of the theory of Universal Grammar. In particular, the Conservative Learning model rejects the claim that children possess innate knowledge of universal linguistic principles. At the earliest stages of language development, on this model, children only produce linguistic expressions that they have experienced in the input. At the earliest stages of language development, children's competence is strictly item-based: children only use the particular expressions to which they are exposed in the way they have heard them.

The Conservative Learning model advanced by Tomasello (2000) also proposes some mechanisms that allow children to go beyond the input. These mechanisms do not make reference to the abstract principles that linguists use in their accounts of adult languages, however. In particular, these mechanisms do not make use of the syntactic organization that linguists assume. This is how Tomasello (2000; p. 214) puts it:

> "Other than the category of nominals, nascent language learners possess no other linguistic abstractions or forms of syntactic organization."

One syntax-blind mechanism that allows children to go beyond the input is *noun substitution*. Children can produce utterances that they have never heard before, but the utterances that children produce only differ from the ones they have encountered in the nominals that children use. By way of illustration, suppose the child hears a sentence like (40).

(40)   John broke the window.

The child will be able to produce utterances like (41), in which the noun phrase *John* has been replaced by *Mary*.

(41)   Mary broke the window.

However, Tomasello (2000) argues, the child will not be able to produce utterances like (42), which involve a different 'template.'

(42)   The window broke.

It is difficult to underestimate the challenge provided by the Conservative Learning model. On this model, not only do children differ from adults in the details of their linguistic competence, but children also differ from adults in the most fundamental aspects of language. Child language and adult language are based on different primitive notions, on this model. If so, the generative study of language acquisition must be inherently flawed. Tomasello (2000) is quite explicit in saying that a generative account is not needed to explain child grammars.

> "Overall, children's limited creativity with their early language calls into question the practice of describing their underlying syntactic competence in terms of abstract and adult-like syntactic categories, schemas and grammars."
> Tomasello (2000; p. 11)

The Conservative Learning model attempts to explain both children's adult-like and non-adult-like productions. Let us focus on one example of the latter. Two-year-olds who are in the process of learning English advance through a stage where they produce infinitival verb forms in root clauses; examples are *He open it* and *She eat grapes* (e.g., Rizzi, 1994; Wexler, 1994; Hoekstra and Hyams, 1998). According to Tomasello (2000), this phenomenon can be explained by observing that children frequently encounter adult questions like *Should he open it?*, *Does she eat grapes?*, and so on. The Conservative Learning model maintains that children produce so-called Root Infinitives because they omit the initial verbal element from the corresponding adult questions. So, for example, the adult's question *Should he open it?* becomes *He open it* in the child's production.

In a preliminary assessment of the Conservative Learning model, Meroni, Gualmini and Crain (2001) argued that this model cannot explain many of the documented mismatches between children and adults.[21] Let us review Meroni et al.'s evaluation of the Conservative Learning model as it pertains to children's production of the non-finite forms we just described. As noted, Tomasello (2000) argues that English-speaking children produce uninflected verb forms by truncating utterances they encounter in the linguistic environment. A natural question is whether adults' utterances are an equally good source of children's truncated constructions in all languages. As a case study, Meroni et al. consider the production of non-finite forms in child German and conjecture that utterances like (43) documented by Poeppel and Wexler (1993) could result from the truncation of adult utterances like (44).

(43) a.   Thorsten   Caesar   haben.
            Thorsten   C.(=doll)   have $_{-finite}$
            'Thorsten has Caesar'
      b.   du   das   haben.
            you   that   have $_{-finite}$
            'you have that'

(44) a.   will   Thorsten   Caesar   haben?
            wants   Thorsten   C.(=doll)   have $_{-finite}$
            'Does Thorsten want to have Caesar?'
      b.   willst   du   das   haben?
            want$_{-2sg}$ you   that   have $_{-finite}$
            'do you want to have that?'

The syntax-blind truncation story, however, would predict that children could also form truncated utterances based on adult utterances such as (45), which are likely to be available in the input.

(45) a.   Mami   sagt   daß   du   ins Bett gehen mußt.
            Mom   says   that   you   to bed   to go must$_{2sg}$
            'Mom says you must go to bed'

---

21 See also Wexler (2002) for discussion of Tomasello's proposal.

b.　　Mami　fragt　was　du　eßen willst.

Mom　asks　what　you　to eat want$_{2sg}$

'Mom asks what you want to eat'

If so, children should produce (some truncated variant of) sentences like those in (46), in which a finite verb occurs in final position.

(46)　a.　　Du　ins Bett gehen mußt.

you　to bed　to go　must$_{2sg}$

'you must go to bed'

b.　　Du　eßen　willst.

You　to eat　want$_{2sg}$

'You want to eat'

This expectation is not borne out, however. Poeppel and Wexler (1993) analyzed the spontaneous speech production of a 2-year-old German-speaking child. The findings show that finiteness and verb position are nearly perfectly correlated; the German-speaking child never produced a non-finite verb followed by a finite form. Moreover, occurrences of a finite verb in any position other than second position are extremely rare.

A second problem with the truncation hypothesis was raised by Meroni et al. (2001). This is the existence of child languages that do not produce non-finite forms in finite contexts. It has been observed that children learning Italian (Guasti, 1994) and Spanish (Grinstead, 1994) do not use non-finite forms in root clauses. Presumably, children who are in the process of learning these languages encounter sentences equivalent to the German examples in (44). Thus, one would expect to find non-finite forms in the speech of children exposed to Italian and Spanish, contrary to fact.

The study by Meroni et al. focuses on cases in which children seem to make some distinctions that are not evident in the input. In the present study, we put aside children's production and we focus on their interpretation.[22] By focusing

---

22 Having outlined the Conservative Learning model, a caveat is in order. Tomasello (2000) maintains that the Conservative Learning model only applies to the process of language acquisition before the child turns three. Tomasello (2000) does not say what happens when the child turns three, however. This is rather unfortunate, as most robust techniques for experimental studies with children are often difficult to carry out with children younger than three. Furthermore, our main concern is to see whether children ever get distracted by the idiosyncrasies in the way entailment relations are

on language interpretation, one can assess children's competence with sentences that they might not have even heard. Furthermore, by focusing on experimental studies of language comprehension one can isolate specific facts that only make sense from the point of view of linguistic theory. One of these phenomena is structure dependence, a by-product of syntactic organization. Structure dependence will also be relevant for a different model of language acquisition to be introduced shortly. The relevant empirical evidence will be presented in Chapter 3. Before we end our discussion of the Conservative Learning model, we would like to recall a different quirk of entailment relations.

For the present purposes, it is important to observe that downward entailment provides a useful case to investigate the mistakes predicted by the Conservative Learning model. As we have just seen, the conservative learning model maintains that children can go *minimally* beyond the input. One mechanism that allows children to go beyond the input is noun substitution. This makes downward entailment an interesting phenomenon, since different noun phrases generate different patterns of entailment. For example, the three sentences in (47) differ in the entailments that they license.

(47)   a.   Every student wrote a paper.
        b.   No student wrote a paper.
        c.   Some student wrote a paper.

Notice that all the sentences in (47) are grammatical. Thus they are all possible utterances in the linguistic input to which the child is exposed. Interestingly, the sentences in (47) only differ in the nominal in subject position. These nominals cannot be freely substituted, however. In fact, the constructions in (47) differ in the licensing of negative polarity items and in the entailment relations that they generate, as shown below.

(48)   a.   *Every student wrote any paper.
        b.   No student wrote any paper.
        c.   *Some student wrote any paper.

---

manifested in natural language. Presumably, older children have encountered *more* data that could lead them to form wrong generalizations. For these reasons, we are compelled to disregard Tomasello's assumption that there are qualitative changes in child language after age three.

(49)   a.   Every student wrote a paper <u>or</u> made a presentation
                       *⇒   Every student wrote a paper <u>and</u> every student made a presentation.

       b.   No student wrote a paper <u>or</u> made a presentation
                       ⇒   No student wrote a paper <u>and</u> no student made a presentation.

       c.   Some student wrote a paper <u>or</u> made a presentation
                       *⇒   Some student wrote a paper <u>and</u> some student made a presentation.

Assuming that a child could freely substitute one nominal with the other, the question is how far the child will draw the parallelism between the three nominals under consideration. This issue will be addressed in Chapter 2.

1.3.2 The Rich Input Model

In a recent evaluation of the poverty of the stimulus argument, Pullum and Scholz (2002) focused on a different assumption of the UG model of language acquisition. In contrast to Tomasello (2000), who denied that children possess the linguistic competence that the UG view attributes them, Pullum and Scholz argued that the flaw of most UG based research lies in the assumption that the input is impoverished. If one looks carefully enough, Pullum and Scholz (2002) argued, the input can be found to provide all the evidence that children need to acquire a natural language, without any assistance from Universal Grammar.

It is important to stress that Pullum and Scholz do not provide a model of language acquisition. Rather, they are concerned with the characterization of the input endorsed by most generative linguistics. If their criticism is correct, however, it should be possible to develop a model of language acquisition that exploits the information available in the input. We call this hypothetical model the Rich Input model.

Despite some important differences, the Conservative Learning model proposed by Tomasello (2000) and the Rich Input model implicit in Pullum and Scholz (2002) shoot at the same target, the UG model of language acquisition. In particular, Pullum and Scholz are concerned with the source of the language specific knowledge that children have. Here is how Pullum and Scholz (2002) put it.

"Certainly, humans are endowed with some sort of predisposition toward language learning. The substantive issue is whether a full description of that predisposition incorporates anything that entails specific contingent facts about natural languages." (Pullum and Scholz, 2002; p. 10)

In their discussion of the poverty of the stimulus argument, Pullum and Scholz (2002) consider a variety of linguistic phenomena, from question formation to noun compounding. Across all these phenomena, the conclusion reached by Pullum and Scholz is that the input provides children with sufficient information.

In Chapter 2, we will argue that the Rich Input model can only account for (some of) the forms that children produce and for (some of) the meanings they assign. What the Rich Input model cannot explain is why children never produce certain forms or assign certain meanings. Of course, one could hypothesize that these forms (and meanings) are not present in the input to which children are exposed and that this explains why children never produce those forms (or assign those meanings). Children eventually have to go beyond the forms and meanings to which they are exposed, however. Children have to come up with generalizations that allow them to produce and interpret forms they have encountered as well as novel forms. The question is how they can do so without incurring in any wrong generalizations.

In order to solve this problem, Pullum and Scholz (2002) could rely on some form of indirect negative evidence. In other words, they could rely on some mechanism that would lead children to consider each sentence they hear as the *only* possible form to convey a particular message. Thus, the grammaticality of one form would 'suggest' the ungrammaticality of all other forms. Once we turn to language comprehension, however, this learning mechanism would have to be complicated considerably. Suppose the child encounters a sentence and somehow manages to decipher the relevant meaning. Given the pervasiveness of semantic ambiguity, no principle should lead the child to assume that the same sentence could not have any other meanings. Thus, the study of language comprehension allows us to sidestep a potential confound of language production.

We would like to focus on the criticism of Pullum and Scholz (2002) offered by Crain and Pietroski (2002). Crain and Pietroski focus on two shortcomings of the Rich Input model. First, the Rich Input model, like the Conservative Learning model, maintains that children entertain shallow linguistic representations, which are *qualitatively* different from those entertained by adults. In Chapter 3 we will consider this issue, by focusing on structure dependence in child language. A related concern expressed by Crain and Pietroski has to do with children's ability to capture generalizations across disparate phenomena. We would like to focus on this second criticism by Crain and Pietroski (2002), mainly because these researchers draw upon the same phenomena that we consider.

In our introduction of downward entailment, we highlighted the correlation between three different phenomena: the licensing of inferences from a set to its subsets, the licensing of negative polarity items and the conjunctive interpretation of the disjunction operator *or*. According to Crain and Pietroski (2002), a generalization hides beneath these seemingly unrelated phenomena and the pervasiveness of this generalization in the adult languages is unanticipated if children can entertain different generalizations during the language acquisition process.[23] We agree with the logic of the Crain and Pietroski argument, but we would like to be more explicit about which generalizations are excluded from the child's hypothesis space.

The model of language acquisition endorsed by Crain and Pietroski will be introduced in the next section. We would like to note here that according to this model, differences between child and adult language are constrained by Universal Grammar. Thus, one needs to consider the constraints imposed by UG on the role of entailment relations for natural languages. For present purposes, it is worth noting that languages differ with respect to what phenomena are sensitive to entailment relations. As a consequence, languages differ with respect to what phenomena are correlated. For instance, languages differ in the kind of expressions that are negative polarity items. Similarly, languages differ in the kind of distinctions that they draw among the set of polarity items. Finally, languages differ in the extent to which the disjunction operator *or* receives a conjunctive interpretation (see Szabolcsi, 2002b). Thus, it would be possible for children to differ from adults with respect to many of the phenomena considered by Crain and Pietroski (2002). In turn, it is possible that children differ from adults in what the relevant generalization is. In fact, it would be quite surprising if this was not the case, since children would have to map the particular sounds of their language onto the appropriate meanings. Considering the model endorsed by Crain and Pietroski (2002), however, the prediction is that children might differ from adults only in those limited ways.

---

23 One of the phenomena considered by Crain and Pietroski (2002) is the cancellation of scalar implicatures (see Chierchia, 2002). On the interaction between scalar implicatures and downward entailment in child language see Gualmini, Crain, Meroni, Chierchia and Guasti (2001).

For example, children might differ from adults in whether the disjunction operator *or* receives a conjunctive interpretation in negative sentences. Whatever generalization they draw, however, children should follow the same structure dependent principles that characterize adult grammars.

1.3.3 The Continuity Assumption

The Continuity Assumption, together with most current research within the generative framework, endorses the assumption that the initial and the final stage of the language acquisition process are constrained by Universal Grammar. In addition to that assumption, the Continuity Assumption maintains that UG assists children throughout the entire course of language acquisition. According to the Continuity Assumption, child language is only expected to differ from the language of the local community in certain limited respects (see Crain and Thornton, 1998; Crain and Pietroski, 2001). Children's grammar may license constructions (or interpretations) that are not attested in the local language, but Universal Grammar constrains the possible mismatches between child language and the target language. Thus, "children's developing grammars can differ from the adult grammar of the linguistic community only in ways in which adult grammars can differ from each other."[24] However, children never entertain linguistic principles that exceed the boundary conditions (i.e., violate any core principles) imposed by Universal Grammar.

The first formulation of the Continuity Assumption is due to MacNamara (1982). MacNamara's work is mainly concerned with word learning, but the relevant claim is presented for children's cognitive development in general.[25] This is how MacNamara presents it:

> "That the mind is ready-made is the null hypothesis: there is no structural difference between the adult and the infant mind; therefore the researcher's task is to reject the null hypothesis. That is standard procedure in science and indeed in psychology. For the rest, I am not at all convinced by the evidence so far produced that this null hypothesis is false." MacNamara (1982; pp. 233-234)

In the domain of language development, the Continuity Assumption was more explicitly formulated by Pinker (1984).

---

24 Crain and Thornton (1998; p. 37).
25 See Carey and Xu (1999) for a discussion of MacNamara's position.

"In sum, I propose that the continuity assumption be applied to accounts of children's language in three ways: in the qualitative nature of child's abilities, in the formal nature of the child's grammatical rules, and in the way that those rules are realized in comprehension and production." Pinker (1984; p. 8)

More recently, the Continuity Assumption has been developed by Crain and Thornton (1998) and Crain and Pietroski (2001).

"There are heavy constraints on the different forms that children's grammars can take, however. The model adopts the Continuity Hypothesis – the claim that children's developing grammars can differ from the adult grammar of the linguistic community only in ways in which adult grammars can differ from each other." Crain and Thornton (1998; p. 37)

When we discussed the Conservative Learning model proposed by Tomasello (2000), we observed that this model attempts to explain children's adult-like productions without attributing adult-like underlying competence to children. As we will see throughout the following chapters, this guiding principle has been followed to a larger extent than is usually recognized. In several cases, children have been argued to differ from adults even when their productions look adult-like. The Continuity Assumption takes the opposite view. Children do not differ from adults in their grammars, on this view, even when children's productions look non-adult-like.

The Continuity Assumption is supported by the finding that young children occasionally produce sentences that are not acceptable in the target language, but are grammatical in some adult languages. For example, some English-speaking children produce *Wh*-questions that are attested in many languages, but not in adult English. That is, some children produce an 'extra' copy of a bare *Wh*-phrase in long-distance questions, as in (50).

(50)   *What do you think what that is?

As in other natural languages, however, English-speaking children who produce questions like (50) refrain from reproducing 'extra' *Wh*-phrases with lexical content, as in (51)a, and these children also fail to reproduce a bare *Wh*-phrase when the extraction site is inside an infinitival clause, as in (51)b (see Thornton, 1990).[26]

---

26 We use the symbol '#' for utterances that were unattested in children's speech.

(51)   a.   #*Which boy do you think which boy that is?
         b.   #*Who do you want who to win?

This pattern of attested and unattested productions is difficult to explain on models of language development in which child language is securely tied to the child's linguistic experience, as in the case of the Conservative Learning model or the Rich Input model. On the other hand, the findings represent circumstantial evidence in favor of the Continuity Assumption. In absence of exposure to cross-linguistic data, the observation that children project beyond their experience in certain ways and not in other ways suggests that children know more about language than they could possibly have learned from experience.

The line of research inaugurated by Thornton (1990) thus lends support to the claim that the observed mismatches between children and adults are compatible with UG. A related line of research explores the issue of never occurring mismatches between children and adults of any linguistic community. This is where the property of downward entailment is relevant. Intuitively, some of the properties related to downward entailment seem easier to detect than others. For example, the distribution of negative polarity items is more easily 'observable' than entailment relations. From the language learner's perspective, the correlation between negative polarity items and entailment properties constitutes an important factor. The language learner could use the distribution of negative polarity items to classify linguistic contexts in two classes. In other words, one could hypothesize that the child learns what contexts are downward entailing on the basis of the distributional evidence available to her, namely the distribution of NPIs. Under this view, the child would scan the input for distributional regularities. On this conservative model of language learning, at any given moment of language development the hypotheses entertained by the child would be constrained by the kind of evidence encountered by the language learner up to that moment. Appealing as it may be, this view ignores two important aspects of downward entailment: the fact that DE contexts also share other linguistic properties, and the relationship between the meaning of an expression and the kinds of entailments the expression generates. Let us consider each of these properties in turn.

The distinction between downward entailing and *non*-downward entailing environments is part of the linguistic knowledge that the child eventually acquires. What the child has to learn, however, is not merely a classification between two or more (classes of) contexts. The child acquires the distinction between DE and *non*-DE environments and the whole range of properties that correlate with this distinction. The distribution of negative polarity items could lead the 'conservative' child to the correct classification between DE and *non-DE* contexts. From the child's perspective, however, the relevance of this classification would not initially extend beyond the distribution of negative polarity items. As a consequence, if children approached the acquisition of downward entailment in a conservative fashion, we would expect that at an early stage of language development they would behave like adults with respect to one property of DE (i.e., the licensing of negative polarity items), but not with respect to some other property of downward entailment (e.g., the generation of entailments in accordance with the De Morgan's law). As we just saw, this is the point raised by Crain and Pietroski (2002).

An independent concern is the acquisition of entailment relations themselves, e.g., the relevant De Morgan's law. It is conceivable, of course, that a child masters the relevant entailment relations among sentences only upon encountering the relevant input. In this case, presumably, the relevant input would consist of pairs of sentences accompanied by a specific indication of the relationship that holds between them (e.g., *If none of the students wrote a paper or made a presentation then none of the students wrote a paper and none of the students made a presentation*). Data of this kind are highly unlikely to be available in sufficient quantity to ensure that all young children encounter them, and thereby master the property of downward entailment early in life. Thus, the conservative view seemingly leads to the prediction that some children at least will not master the property of downward entailment early in the course of language development.

Although logically possible, this outcome is highly implausible. To see what children actually learn, one needs to consider the relationship between the meaning of a linguistic expression and the entailment relationships such an expression generates.

The property of downward entailment is closely related to the meaning of certain linguistic expressions across natural languages. Let us illustrate with an example. The relationship between the meaning of a determiner and the direction of the entailment relationships of its restrictor and its nuclear scope becomes easier to grasp if we consider the meaning of a determiner as a relationship between the set denoted by its restrictor and the set denoted by its nuclear scope. Consider a sentence like (52).

(52)   No student wrote any paper.

The sentence in (52) is true if the set of students and the set of individuals who wrote a paper generate an empty intersection. Now, consider the sentences in (53), in which we restrict the denotation of the noun phrase *student* and that of the verb phrase *wrote a paper* to a subset of their denotation in (52).

(53)   a.   No first year student wrote any paper.
        b.   No student wrote any good paper.

If (52) is true, both sentences in (53) are also true. This is hardly surprising, however. If (52) is true, it means that we are dealing with two sets generating an empty intersection. Reducing the 'size' of the set of students or the set of individuals who wrote a paper will not produce any change in the intersection between those two sets. A change could only arise from an *increase* in the set picked out by the restrictor or by the nuclear scope.

Since the pattern of entailments that an expression generates is determined by its meaning, one cannot ask how a child might learn the former without considering how she could learn the latter. It is therefore misleading to ask how a child might learn that, for example, both the restrictor and the nuclear scope of the determiner *no* are downward entailing without first considering how the child might learn the meaning of the determiner *no*. The entailment relationship displayed by the determiner *no* is not an accidental property of the determiner *no*. Rather, the entailment relations of a determiner directly follow from the meaning of that determiner. As we will discuss in Chapter 4, some models of language acquisition maintain that the acquisition of determiner meanings is largely determined in advance, by Universal Grammar. If so, it follows that only a small set of the possibly infinite hypotheses about determiner meanings can be entertained by the child. Under this hypothesis, we expect children's knowledge of downward entailment to be essentially adult-like from the earliest stages of language development, as soon as children map the correct meaning onto the particular sound that their language provides. In particular, we expect children to be like adults in the classification of a linguistic context as DE or *non*-DE, since natural languages do not differ in this respect. Children might differ from adults, however, with respect to the items classified as negative polarity items, since natural languages *do* differ in this classification.

As we observed in the last section, Crain and Pietroski (2002) argue that, in the particular case at hand, children and adults should converge on the same generalizations. This does not exclude the possibility that children might entertain different generalizations during the language acquisition process, as long as the differences between children and adults do not exceed the boundaries of Universal Grammar. It is possible that children go through a stage where the word *any* is not subject to the same restrictions of the adult language. For example, a child might initially assume that *any* is subject to the same licensing condition of the negative polarity item *yet*, and this would not exceed the boundaries of UG. Similarly, it is possible that children go through a stage in which they interpret (sentences containing) the word *or* differently from adults in the relevant environment. For example, a child learning Hungarian or Japanese might incorrectly assume the disjunction operator can be interpreted in the scope of downward entailing operators, despite the fact that the target language does not exploit this possibility. Whatever generalization the child might be forming, however, children and adults should not differ with respect to the primitives that are needed to express that generalization.

For the sake of the argument, suppose that English-speaking children go through a stage in which *some* is a negative polarity item. Then these children will most likely use the word *some* in a subset of the downward entailing environments. Children might even assume that *some* must occur in the scope of negation, but it cannot occur in the scope of the quantifier *few*. Even in this non-adult scenario, however, one should be able to see the blueprint of Universal Grammar. For example, one should be able to show that *some* is licensed by (a subset of) downward entailing operators under some structural configuration. Against the background of all the incorrect hypotheses that children could possibly make, the Continuity Assumption maintains that some other hypotheses would never be considered. For instance, children should never hypothesize that the mere presence of negation licenses the occurrence of *some*. Although children might differ from adults in how they classify the word *some*, they should not differ from adults in what the relevant notion of scope is.

1.4 Conclusion

The purpose of the present chapter was to introduce one property, which is implicated in many phenomena across natural languages. In presenting these phenomena we have highlighted those features that are most surprising from a pre-theoretical point of view. In turn, we have argued that the relevance of these features differs depending on what model of language acquisition one considers. In the remainder of the present dissertation, we investigate some of the quirks of downward entailment in more detail.

CHAPTER 2

Entailment and Polarity Phenomena in Child Language

The first chapter introduced three alternative models of language acquisition and one specific phenomenon that we will use in assessing these models. The present chapter looks at downward entailment from the viewpoint of child language. First, we review previous research on children's knowledge of linguistic phenomena related to downward entailment. The main focus of previous research on children's knowledge of downward entailment lies in the licensing conditions and the interpretation of negative polarity items. Therefore, an additional feature must be brought into the picture before we can draw on children's knowledge of downward entailment for the purposes set forth in Chapter 1. This phenomenon is related to the interpretation of the disjunction operator *or* in the scope of downward entailing operators. We present an experimental investigation of children's interpretation of the disjunction operator *or* in the scope of the quantified expression *None of the Ns*. The relevance of the findings is threefold. First, the findings expand our understanding of children's knowledge of polarity phenomena. In particular, they highlight children's knowledge of one interpretive consequence of downward entailment. Second, the findings illustrate how comprehension studies can be used to tap into children's knowledge of downward entailment by providing us with a criterion of downward entailment, which can be exploited in further experimental studies. Third, the findings allow us to introduce the role of felicity conditions in child language, which will be discussed further in Chapters 4 and 5.

2.1 Polarity Phenomena in Child Language

Research on children's knowledge of downward entailment has mainly focused on the licensing conditions and the interpretation of the negative polarity item *any*. Children's knowledge of the licensing conditions of *any* was first investigated by O'Leary and Crain (1994). These researchers conducted an Elicited Production task with 11 children (ages: 4;4 to 5;4) in an experiment designed to evoke downward entailing and *non*-downward entailing environments in children's productions.[1] The Elicited Production task is an experimental technique that is used to provide children with the most appropriate context to produce a particular structure, without providing them with any instance of that structure. In the case at hand, the task was designed to make it appropriate for children to produce affirmative and negative sentences. In order to evoke a downward entailing context like negation, for example, one experimenter acted out a short story about some dogs. Some of the dogs were very hungry and eventually found some food. However, one dog decided not to eat any food. At this point, a puppet manipulated by a second experimenter uttered the target sentence in (1), which children consistently rejected.

(1)   Every dog got some food.

Children were then encouraged to explain to the puppet "what really happened in the story?" This was the elicitation part of the experiment, which provided the relevant finding. In accordance with the licensing conditions of the NPI *any* in the adult grammar, children often used the negative polarity item *any* in the scope of negation in their response, uttering sentences like (2).

(2)   No, this dog did not get any food!

It bears observing that some children occasionally offered sentences like (3) as a justification for their rejection of the target sentence.

---

1 See Thornton (1996) and Crain and Thornton (1998) for a detailed description of the Elicited Production technique.

(3)   *No, this dog did not get some food![2]

Thus, some children resorted to (3) to convey the interpretation that adults reserve to (2).

The findings of the first experimental condition of the Crain et al. study show that children's grammar licenses the occurrence of the negative polarity item *any* in negative sentences. In fact, children show a preference towards the use of *any* over *some* in negative contexts, although the use of *some* is not completely ruled out by all children's grammars.

Let us turn to the experimental condition, which was designed to evoke *non*-DE contexts. In one of the trials, children were presented with a story in which every dog ate some food. In this context, the puppet's description was (4).

(4)   Only one dog got any food.

In this condition, children rejected the target sentence uttered by the puppet, and described what really happened in the story by using sentences like (5).

(5)   No, every dog got some food!

Importantly, sentences like (6), in which *any* lacks a proper licensor, were almost unattested in children's responses.

(6)   *No, every dog got any food!

In other words, children refrained from using *any* in upward entailing contexts, such as the nuclear scope of the universal quantifier *every*, despite the fact that they had just heard the word *any* in the puppet's statement.

The findings of the O'Leary and Crain study suggest that 4-year-old children use the negative polarity item *any* in downward entailing contexts, but refrain from doing so in upward entailing contexts. The same adult-like pattern does not emerge for the positive polarity item *some*. In fact, children used *some* in both downward and upward entailing environments, although they showed a preference for the latter kind of environment, thereby showing a *tendency* towards the adult pattern.

---

2 The utterance in (3) is ungrammatical – or at least strongly dispreferred - on the intended interpretation, i.e., *No, this dog did not get any food* (see Ladusaw, 1979).

Another study on polarity phenomena in child language was conducted by van der Wal (1996), who used an Imitation task, as well as a Grammaticality Judgment task. The findings of the study by van der Wal (1996) were consistent with the results obtained by O'Leary and Crain (1994). Dutch-speaking children possessed knowledge of negative polarity items from the earliest stages of language development (see also Koster and van der Wal, 1995). In particular, van der Wal (1996) focused on two common NPIs in Dutch: the modal verb *hoeven (have to/need)* and the adverb *meer (anymore)*. The findings suggest that children know that these items are subject to a stricter distribution than ordinary verbs or temporal adverbs from the early stages of language development. Young children differ from adults, however, in that they still have to figure out what contexts count as 'negative' contexts. Thus, according to van der Wal (1996), the acquisition of the restrictions on negative polarity items boils down to the process of acquiring the different ways to express 'negative' meanings.

So far we have focused on the licensing conditions on the use of polarity terms in child language. Of course, this does not take into account the interpretive consequences of downward entailment. To complete the picture, we turn to two comprehension studies of the interpretation of *any* and *some*. The first was a study by Thornton (1994), who investigated children's awareness of the difference in meaning between questions like (7) and (8).

(7)   Did<u>n't</u> <u>any</u> of the turtles buy an apple?

(8)   Did <u>any</u> of the turtles <u>not</u> buy an apple?

It is important to notice that, in (7), *any* is interpreted as an existential quantifier within the scope of negation. In (8), by contrast, *any* is interpreted as an existential quantifier which takes scope over negation. The responses collected by Thornton (1994) show that children as young as 3;6 discriminate between these two interpretations. In the experiment, children were asked the questions in (7) and (8) in a context in which two turtles had bought an apple and a third turtle had not bought any apple. Thornton (1994) found that children younger than four would respond "yes" in response to (7) and point to the two turtles that had bought an apple, but they would respond "yes" and point to the turtle that had *not* bought any apple in response to (8). Thus, the findings suggest that children's interpretation of *any* is sensitive to the different order with which this item and negation occur in (7) and (8).

Let us now turn to positive polarity items. As we mentioned, children's use of the positive polarity item *some* documented by O'Leary and Crain did not conform to the target grammar to the same extent as their use of *any*. This result was further investigated by Musolino (1998) in a Truth Value Judgment task. The Truth Value Judgment is an experimental technique that allows one to investigate whether a specific interpretation of a target sentence is licensed by the child's grammar (Crain and McKee, 1985; Crain and Thornton, 1998). In a Truth Value Judgment task, there are typically two experimenters. One experimenter acts out short stories in front of the child, using props and toys. Each story constitutes a context against which the child evaluates one of the target sentences, which is uttered by a puppet that is being manipulated by a second experimenter. The acceptance of the target sentence is interpreted as indicating that the target sentence can receive an interpretation that is true in the context under consideration. By contrast, the rejection of the target sentence is interpreted as suggesting that the child's grammar does not license any interpretation that makes the target sentence true in the context under consideration.[3]

The relevant experiment conducted by Musolino (1998) focused on sentences like (9).

(9)   The detective didn't find some guys.[4]

Sentence (9) was presented as a description of a context in which the detective had only succeeded in finding two of the four guys mentioned in the story. The context employed by Musolino (1998) was designed to make (9) true on its adult interpretation (i.e., the interpretation paraphrased in (10)), in which *some* does not occur in the scope of negation), and false on its non-adult interpretation (i.e., the interpretation paraphrased in (11), in which *some* occurs in the scope of negation).

(10)   There are some guys that the detective didn't find.

(11)   It is not the case that the detective found some guys.

---

3 As we will see in Chapters 4 and 5, the experimental design must take into account all the contextual factors that may affect the interpretation under consideration, both for children and adults.

4 Recall that adults tend to assign wide scope to the indefinite *some* in sentences like (9), thereby accepting the sentence as long as some guys were not found.

The finding was that children as old as 5;9 rejected the target sentences, whereas the adult controls consistently accepted them. In particular, many of the children interviewed by Musolino (1998) pointed out that (9) was incorrect because the detective had indeed found some guys. Apparently, children's rejection of (9) followed from the interpretation in (11), an interpretation that the adult grammar does not license for (9).

To recap, the findings from previous research on children's interpretation of indefinites in negative sentences lead to a confusing picture. Children's production and interpretation of the negative polarity item *any* conforms to the adult grammar, but their production and interpretation of the indefinite *some* does not appear to reflect adult competence. The difference in the interpretation of *some* and *any* in negative sentences is not the only difference between these two expressions. On some linguistic accounts, however, the interpretation of the indefinite *some* outside the scope of negation is closely related to the availability of the negative polarity item *any*. The clearest example of this approach is provided by Krifka (1995), who derives the wide scope interpretation of the indefinite *some* through a pragmatic reasoning that starts from the availability of *any* (to convey the narrow scope interpretation). This analysis makes the pattern provided by child language even more surprising. We return to this puzzle in Chapter 5. For the time being, we would like to sidestep the issues raised by the available evidence on children's knowledge of polarity phenomena and focus on some issues that have not been addressed.

2.2 The Boundaries of the Current Picture

In Chapter 1 we set forth an ambitious goal. We proposed to look at one specific linguistic phenomenon, hoping that we would learn something about how grammar formation takes place. Despite the existence of several experimental studies, we have only begun to approach our goal. There are two related limitations to the picture that we have described so far. The first limitation has to do with the phenomenon itself, while the second limitation has to do with experimental methodology.

The studies that we have reviewed so far only looked at the most easily observable consequence of downward entailment, namely the distribution of items that are restricted to downward entailing environments. Moreover, the experimental methodology adopted by those studies only allows us to conclude what form (or meaning) is licensed by the child's grammar. That methodology, however, can hardly be used to reach any conclusion about what forms or meanings are not licensed by the child's grammar. As an example, recall the O'Leary and Crain study. These researchers conducted an Elicited Production task. The finding was that children used the negative polarity item *any* in negative contexts, but children avoided it in positive contexts. Unfortunately, this does not authorize us to conclude that the same children would find ungrammatical the use of the negative polarity item *any* lacking a proper licensor if they were asked to evaluate a sentence like (12):

(12)   *No, every dog got any food!

At most, the findings by O'Leary and Crain (1994) suggest that children might disprefer the use of negative polarity items in positive sentences, where they prefer *some*.[5] Unfortunately, no experimental methodology can overcome this problem, although some tasks seem to be more reliable than others.[6]

     A more serious concern comes from the specific phenomena investigated by O'Leary and Crain (1994). It is hard to come up with an evaluation metric that would make the findings that we have presented surprising. Any input-based model would predict them. Up to this point, children could give the responses collected by O'Leary and Crain (1994), if they only used the word *any* in the contexts in which they have witnessed the word *any*. On this view, children do not produce sentences like (12), because they have never heard anything similar to those sentences.

     There is a way out of this impasse, however. One possibility is to expand the range of phenomena under consideration. In particular, one could include sentences that look like the sentences in the O'Leary and Crain study in some respects, but still differ with respect to downward entailment. For example, one could extend the O'Leary and Crain study by eliciting sentences containing

---

     5 It is worth recalling that children avoided the term used by the puppet. By inference, one could argue that the use of that term would have been unacceptable. Still, the data collected by van der Wal (1996) suggest that different experimental techniques might yield a less clear pattern than the one documented by O'Leary and Crain (1994). Similarly, the findings documented by Musolino (1998) suggest that children might differ from adults in their interpretation of the positive polarity item *some* to a larger extent than suggested by the O'Leary and Crain study.

     6 In principle, this difficulty could be overcome if one conducted a Grammaticality Judgment task. However, Grammaticality Judgment tasks arguably involve a metalinguistic component that makes them unfit for young children (for discussion, see McDaniel and Cairns, 1996).

negation and indefinites in different structural configurations. A second possibility is to shift the focus on language comprehension. Thus, one can ask children to interpret pairs of sentences that differ with respect to the relevant property but do not differ with respect to the possibility of occurring in the input. A study by Boster and Crain (1993) constitutes a first step in this direction.

The study by Boster and Crain (1993) introduces an important feature. These researchers used a comprehension task which allows the experimenter to focus on meaning. Boster and Crain (1993) focus on a specific linguistic phenomenon whose interaction with downward entailment manifests itself at the level of the interpretation, rather than at the level of grammaticality. In particular, Boster and Crain (1993) investigated children's interpretation of sentences containing disjunction in the nuclear scope of the universal quantifier *every*, which is a non-downward entailing environment. The research question addressed in the Boster and Crain study was whether children would extend the application of the relevant De Morgan's law to *non*-DE environments. In order to address this question, Boster and Crain (1993) conducted an experiment employing the Truth Value Judgment task (Crain and Thornton, 1998).

In the Boster and Crain (1993) experiment, children were asked to evaluate sentences like (13) in various scenarios.

(13)   Every ghostbuster will choose a cat or a pig.[7]

The results obtained by Boster and Crain (1993) provide evidence that children do not treat the nuclear scope of the universal quantifier *every* as downward entailing, i.e., children did not interpret (13) as equivalent to (14).

(14)   Every ghostbuster will choose a cat <u>and</u> every ghostbuster will choose a pig.

---

7 The experiment employed the Prediction Mode, a variant of the Truth Value Judgment task described by Chierchia, Crain, Guasti and Thornton (1998). The Prediction Mode differs from the standard Truth Value Judgment task in that the target sentence is presented to the child before the completion of the story, as a prediction about what will happen in the remainder of the story. Since the target sentence is presented before the hearer has all the necessary information to evaluate its truth or falsity, the Prediction Mode can be used whenever the target sentence includes an expression that could trigger a scalar implicatures, e.g., the disjunction operator *or* (see Grice 1975)

In particular, children generally accepted (13) in a context in which every ghostbuster had chosen exactly one object, thereby showing that they were *not* assigning the conjunctive interpretation to the disjunction operator *or*. Thus, the experimental findings show that children do not extend the pattern of inference that characterizes downward entailing environments to the second argument of the universal quantifier *every*, a *non*-DE environment.

Interestingly, Boster and Crain (1993) discovered some non-adult behavior in children's interpretation of the sentences under investigation. As we said, children generally accepted (13) if every ghostbuster had chosen exactly one object. Almost every child, however, imposed an additional restriction on the interpretation of (13). One group of children expected the (kind of) animal chosen by the ghostbusters to be the same for all ghostbusters, and a second group of children expected the (kind of) animal chosen by the ghostbusters *not* to be the same for all ghostbusters.[8] For present purposes, it is important to notice that, despite this non-adult behavior, children did not extend the inference scheme typical of downward entailing environments to the second argument of *every*. Although one would like to have an explanation of the mistakes made by children, this should not lead us to overlook the fact that they failed to make certain other mistakes. In particular, the findings by Boster and Crain suggest that children, like adults, do not assume that the second argument of the universal quantifier *every* constitutes a downward entailing environment. The question is how much linguistic competence is reflected by this simple fact.

Taking stock, we have reviewed various studies on children's knowledge of polarity phenomena. The relevance of these studies differs depending on which model of language acquisition one endorses. A notable exception is constituted by Boster and Crain (1993) who attempted to investigate an 'immediate' consequence of downward entailment. Now, a possible explanation for the findings of that study is that children refrained from assigning the conjunctive interpretation to disjunction for sentences like (13) because they would *never* assign that interpretation. Thus, the findings documented by Boster and Crain (1993) would be even more interesting, if one could show that children *do* sometimes assign the conjunctive interpretation to the disjunction operator, i.e. they do assume that some linguistic environments are downward entailing. At this aim, we turn to an experimental investigation of the quantified expression *None of the Ns*.

---

8 We refer the reader to the original study for a discussion of the experimental results (but see also Chapter 4 for a similar experiment).

2.3 Children's Knowledge of the Logical Properties of Downward Entailment[9]

In this section we turn to the nuclear scope of quantificational phrases of the form *None of the Ns*.[10] The nuclear scope of *None of the Ns* is downward entailing. First, sentences containing a quantified phrase like *None of the Ns* license inferences from a set to its subsets, as shown in (15).

(15)   None of the students have written a <u>paper</u> yet
            ⇒   None of the students have written a <u>good paper</u> yet.

Second, negative polarity items are licensed in the nuclear scope of *None of the Ns*, as shown in (16).

(16)   a.   None of the students wrote <u>any</u> paper.
           b.   None of the students <u>ever</u> wrote a paper.

Finally, the interpretation of sentences containing disjunction in the scope of the quantificational expression *None of the Ns* conforms to the De Morgan's law discussed in Chapter 1.

(17)   None of the students wrote a paper <u>or</u> made a presentation yet
            ⇒   None of the students wrote a paper yet <u>and</u> none of the students made a presentation yet.

Given its downward entailing properties, the nuclear scope of the quantificational phrase *None of the Ns* provides a useful context to address one question that was left unanswered by previous research, namely whether children extend the pattern of entailment of many *non*-downward entailing environments to downward entailing contexts.

---

9 A preliminary report of this study is presented in Gualmini (2001).

10 We will not be concerned with the partitive character of the quantified expression under investigation. The reason we decided to use *None of the Ns* instead of *No* in our study was that the use of the partitive phrase seemed slightly more natural for English speakers in the experimental context.

2.3.1 An Experimental Study on Children's Knowledge of Downward Entailment

This experiment tested children's knowledge of one of the logical properties of downward entailment. As we observed in Chapter 1, the interpretation of (sentences containing) the disjunction operator in the scope of downward entailing operators conforms to the following scheme:

(18) $OP_{DE}(A \text{ or } B) \Rightarrow OP_{DE}(A)$ and $OP_{DE}(B)$

The present experiment was designed to investigate if young children know that the interpretation of the disjunction operator *or* in the scope of the quantified expression *None of the Ns* must conform to the schema in (18). Let us review how (18) models the interpretation of sentences containing the disjunction operator *or* in the scope of *None of the Ns* in English.[11] Consider (19).

(19)   None of the students wrote a paper or made a presentation.

This sentence gives rise to the inference in (20)a, but not to the one in (20)b.

(20)   a.   None of the students wrote a paper <u>or</u> made a presentation
            $\Rightarrow$ None of the students wrote a paper <u>and</u> none
            of the students made a presentation.
        b.   None of the students wrote a paper <u>or</u> made a presentation
            *$\Rightarrow$ None of the students wrote a paper <u>or</u> none
            of the students made a presentation.

It is important to recall that the interpretation of the disjunction operator in the scope of many *non*-DE operators gives rise to the opposite pattern:

(21)   a.   Some of the students wrote a paper <u>or</u> made a presentation
            *$\Rightarrow$ Some of the students wrote a paper, <u>and</u>
            some of the students made a presentation.

---

11 In the case of *None of the Ns*, the converse of (18) is also valid. We will not be concerned with this additional property of the environment under consideration.

b.   Some of the students wrote a paper <u>or</u> made a presentation
⇒   Some of the students wrote a paper <u>or</u> some
of the students made a presentation.

The question is how a child could learn that quantifiers like *None of the Ns* and *Some of the Ns* (or *Every N*, for that matter) generate different entailments. This question becomes all the more relevant if we recall one of the features of the Conservative Learning model proposed by Tomasello (2000). As noted in Chapter 1, this model maintains that children can only go minimally beyond the input they are exposed to. One of the syntax-blind mechanisms that children can resort to is noun substitution. We argued in Chapter 1 that this mechanism cannot explain how children could come to master the difference in the grammaticality of the sentences in (22) or the difference in interpretation of the sentences in (23).

(22)   a.   None of the students wrote <u>any</u> paper.
        b.   *Every student wrote <u>any</u> paper.

(23)   a.   None of the students wrote a paper <u>or</u> made a presentation.
        b.   Every student wrote a paper <u>or</u> made a presentation.

Suppose a child learned how to interpret sentences containing the disjunction operator by generalizing on the basis of other sentences with similar surface forms. If this were the case, then we would expect some children to assign a wrong interpretation to sentences like (23)a or (23)b. In principle, children could make two kinds of mistakes. First, if children happened to see that adults reject (23)a in a situation in which only one of the disjuncts is true, they might do the same with (23)b. Second, children might accept (23)a in a situation in which only one of the disjuncts is true, if they happened to see adults accept (23)b in a situation in which only one of the disjuncts is true. The study by Boster and Crain (1993) suggests that the first mistake does occur, but it does not allow us to draw any conclusion about the second kind mistake.

The scenario envisioned by the Conservative Learning model of language acquisition contrasts with the prediction of the Continuity Assumption. On this view, children's interpretation of sentences like (23)a could conform to the scheme in (18) from the early stages of language acquisition, because that interpretation is UG-compatible. In short, children would not construct a wrong generalization on the basis of the interpretation of *or* in most *non*-DE environments and would use the same interpretation as adults. To distinguish between these two hypotheses, we designed an experiment employing the Truth Value Judgment task.

2.3.2 Experiment I

Let us recall the relevant features of the Truth Value Judgment task (Crain and McKee, 1985; Crain and Thornton, 1998). In a Truth Value Judgment task, one experimenter acts out short stories in front of the child. Each story constitutes a context against which the target sentence, uttered by the puppet manipulated by a second experimenter, is evaluated. In a Truth Value Judgment task, the experimenter constructs a context that distinguishes between the adult interpretation and the non-adult interpretation under investigation. In particular, the optimal design of the Truth Value Judgment task introduces a context that falsifies the adult interpretation of the target sentence and verifies the non-adult interpretation under investigation. This maneuver is motivated by three considerations (see Crain and Thornton, 1998; p. 130). First, it allows the experimenter to ensure that the child rejects the target sentence for the relevant reason (e.g., by asking 'what really happened?'). Second, on the assumption that subjects follow the Gricean Maxim of Charity, these maneuvers make it easier for children to access the non-adult interpretation under investigation, if that is licensed by their grammar. Third, it is normally assumed that subjects respond affirmatively when they are confused (see e.g., Grimshaw and Rosen, 1990). By making the adult interpretation false, one avoids the risk of counting the positive response of subjects who are confused as supporting the experimental hypothesis.

Let us now illustrate the design of the present experiment. In one of the trials, children were told the following story.

(24)   "This is a story about an Indian who is going to shop for groceries. The Indian has heard that some pirates have been surprised stealing in a camp nearby, so he decides to hide all his things before he leaves. In particular he wants to hide three knives, a golden necklace and a jewel. He is really concerned about the jewel and the golden necklace, because he received them as a gift from a dear friend of his. He puts each object in a barrel and then leaves. After he leaves, three pirates arrive. One pirate says: "Look, an Indian camp! There is always a lot of stuff to steal in an Indian camp! I am sure we will find something valuable, like a jewel. Maybe even a golden necklace!" and he takes

one of the barrels. He looks inside and finds a knife. A second pirate says: "Oh, just a knife! Well, I'll see if I can find something better. Maybe I can find a jewel, or maybe I can find a necklace." He takes one barrel, and he finds a knife. The third pirate says: "Oh! you guys were not lucky at all! I am sure there is something better to steal here. I'll go now!" The third pirate takes a third barrel. When he looks inside the barrel, however, he also finds a knife. The pirates are very disappointed, and they are ready to leave because they know the Indian is about to come back. But one pirate says: "Hey, I can't believe we haven't been able to find anything better than knives. I will go back one more time and see what I can find!" He runs back to the Indian camp and he takes another barrel. When he looks inside he finds a jewel, and says: "See! I told you it was worth going back one more time! Now we can leave"."

At this point, the puppet uttered the target sentence, preceded by the linguistic antecedent, as in (25).

(25)   This was a story about an Indian and some pirates and I know what happened. Every pirate found a knife, but <u>none of the pirates found the jewel or the necklace</u>.

Notice that the target sentence is false on the interpretation licensed by the adult grammar (i.e., (26)a), but it is true on the interpretation that is not licensed by the adult grammar, and which could be constructed by analogy from *non*-DE environments (i.e., (26)b).

(26)   a.   None of the pirates found the jewel <u>and</u> none of the pirates found the necklace.
        b.   None of the pirates found the jewel <u>or</u> none of the pirates found the necklace.

If children know the downward entailing properties of the nuclear scope of the partitive phrase *None of the Ns*, they should consistently reject the target sentences.

Thirty children (from age 3;10 to 5;10 - mean age: 4;07) participated in the experiment. Each child was presented with four target trials, preceded by a warm-up trial, and interspersed with filler sentences. In the design of the experiment, we also controlled for a possible order effect of the disjunct that made the target sentence false (on the adult interpretation). So, in two of the trials the sentence was false because of the first disjunct, just as in the story described above; in the remaining two trials, the target sentence was false because of the second disjunct (see the Appendix for details).

Let us look at the results. Out of the 120 trials, children rejected the target sentences 105 times (87.5%). When the children were asked to explain "what really happened in the story?", they consistently pointed out that one of the pirates had actually found the jewel. A control group of 28 English-speaking adults were tested using a video-taped version of the experiment. The adult control group rejected the target sentence 99% of the time.

The findings show that children interpret the disjunction operator in accordance with the relevant De Morgan's law, when *or* occurs in the nuclear scope of the quantified expression *None of the Ns*. Children can indeed assign the conjunctive interpretation to the disjunction operator *or*, when entailment relations warrant this interpretation. Thus, the fact that children do not always assign the conjunctive interpretation to the disjunction operator *or* as shown by Boster and Crain (1993) becomes even more important. Preliminary as the results may be, they provide us with a pattern. This pattern calls for an explanation and the question is what 'primitives' are required by that explanation.

We will pursue our characterization of children's knowledge of downward entailment in the remaining chapters. For the time being, we would like to point out what will *not* be part of our characterization: noun substitution. The data above suggest that noun substitution does not achieve descriptive adequacy – not to mention explanatory adequacy – as it pertains to children's interpretation of sentences containing disjunction. Noun substitution is a very simple mechanism. As such, it might be argued that noun substitution would guide children's interpretation of sentences that are unlikely to have occurred in the input.[12] This did not happen, however. Whatever mechanism children are using to go beyond the input, it has to be considerably more complicated than noun substitution.

It is worth discussing the results of the experiment further. In particular, we would like to speculate on why children's rate of rejection did not reach the percentage that is usually required in a Truth Value Judgment task (i.e., 90%). In (25), the target sentence (e.g., *None of the pirates found the jewel or the necklace*) is preceded by another statement about the story (*Every pirate found a*

---

12 See Crain, Gualmini and Pietroski (2003) for the results of a corpus based search on sentences containing the disjunction operator *or*.

knife). This experimental feature was dictated by children's behavior in the first stage of the execution of the experiment, during which the puppet did not mention what the pirates had found and during which most non-adult responses were recorded. Interestingly, children's unexpected acceptances of the target sentences were often accompanied by a comment about what the characters in the story had done (e.g., "They found a knife!"). In our view, such comments indicated that children were focusing on what had happened in the story, while the target sentence described what had *failed* to happen. Intuitively, children seemed to expect the puppet to describe what the pirates had found, but the target sentence did not fulfill such an expectation. This hypothesis suggested to us that children's non-adult answers were due to the failure to satisfy the felicity conditions associated with a negative statement.[13]

To overcome this potential confounding factor, we introduced a more elaborate linguistic antecedent in the remainder of the experiment. We thought that if the puppet itself had specified that the pirates had found a knife, then the puppet could continue and specify what they had *not* found. In this way, the puppet described the entire content of the story. The results obtained with the (fifteen) children who were presented with the more elaborate linguistic antecedent are consistent with this prediction. The effect of the longer linguistic antecedent can be seen if we compare the responses of the children who were not presented with the elaborate linguistic antecedent (Group I) with the responses of the children who were presented with such antecedent (Group II). Children in Group I (fifteen children ranging in age from 3;10 to 5;10 – mean age 4;07) rejected the target sentence 48 times out of 60 (80%), and children in Group II (fifteen children ranging in age from 4;01 to 5;08 – mean age 4;07) rejected the target sentence 57 times out of 60 (95%). Notice that if the affirmative responses given by (some of) the children in Group I had been dictated by the non-adult interpretation in (25), the use of a longer linguistic antecedent should have made no difference.

---

13 We will discuss the difficulty posed by negative sentences in more detail in Chapter 5. For the time being, it is worth observing that children's interpretation of sentences containing quantified expressions headed by *No* or *None of the Ns* has not been investigated in great detail by previous studies. Previous research on children's understanding of sentences involving negation has not reported this kind of difficulty in children's responses. It is therefore possible that the difficulty experienced by the children who participated in the experiment results from the interaction between the use of a negative-like statement and the particular quantifier involved.

A second issue needs to be addressed. This is the difficulty of the construction under investigation.[14] The target sentences turned out to be quite difficult for the child subjects. On several occasions, after the child had decided whether the puppet was right or wrong, the first experimenter invited the child to repeat what the puppet had said, saying: "Oh you were paying very close attention to this story! I was not listening, so I would like you to tell me what the puppet said about the story." Surprisingly, many children failed to repeat the target sentence uttered by the puppet verbatim, despite their adult-like judgments of the puppet's assertion. Furthermore, most of the children who responded to such a request systematically modified the target sentences, and offered a sentence containing the universal quantifier *every* and negation. To illustrate, if the puppet had produced the target sentence in (27), children were very likely to report his assertion as (28).

(27)   None of the pirates found the jewel or the necklace.

(28)   Every pirate didn't find the jewel or the necklace.

Notice that (27) and (28) are both false in the context set up by the experiment, and in both cases the disjunction operator occurs in a downward entailing environment. Thus, it is difficult to construct a context discriminating between the two interpretations in (27) and (28). Children's tendency to rephrase (27) as (28) is an important finding, however. In particular, it raises a potential puzzle for the current picture of adult languages.

Two issues immediately arise. First, one needs to determine if children's difficulties with quantified expressions of the form *None of the Ns* lead to non-adult behavior in particular contexts. Second, it is important to determine what lies behind children's choice of (28) as a paraphrase of (27) (i.e., why (28) was

---

14 Incidentally, this is one of the reasons why our youngest subject was 3;10. It is important to compare this study with the study by Boster and Crain (1995), which investigated children's knowledge of the logical properties of *non*-DE environments by testing children ranging in age from 3;6 to 6;0, with a mean age of 4;8. As for the study by Conway and Crain, who used the same quantified expressions in their target sentences, they interviewed "fifteen three-to-five year old children" (Conway and Crain, 1995; p. 190). Sentences containing the determiner *no* were also used in an experiment investigating children's knowledge of Principle B conducted by Savarese (1999). The children who participated in the experiment conducted by Savarese (1999) ranged in age from 4;3 to 6;4.

used instead of other possible paraphrases like *There isn't any pirate who found the jewel or the necklace*). As we hinted at above, the use of an existential quantifier in the scope of negation is equivalent to the use of a universal quantifier having scope over negation.

(29) $\neg\exists xP(x) \Leftrightarrow \forall x\neg P(x)$

Despite the logical equivalence illustrated in (29), it has been argued that the two representations do not equally account for the behavior of negative quantifiers in natural languages.

The first relevant observation is due to Kratzer (1995), who concludes that the following German example shows that negative (plural) quantifier phrases should be decomposed into negation and an existential quantifier.

(30)   weil keine Beispiele   bekannt sein müssen
        since no   examples   known be must
        'since no examples must be known'

Kratzer's argument proceeds as follows. If *keine Beispiele* were an ordinary quantifier, we would expect the sentence to be ambiguous depending on the relative scope assignment of *keine Beispiele* and the necessity operator introduced by the modal *müssen*. The two relevant readings would be the ones formalized and paraphrased in (31) and (32).

(31)   a.   no(x) [example(x)] [□ known(x)]
        b.   There is no example, such that it is necessary to know that example.

(32)   a.   □ no(x) [example(x)] [known(x)].
        b.   It is necessary that there be no example that is known.

The sentence in (30) does not have either of these readings, however. Rather, the sentence in (30) only allows the reading represented and paraphrased in (33):

(33)   a.   ¬ □∃(x) [example(x) & known(x)]
        b.   It is not the case that there must be an example that is known.

Thus, the contribution of *keine* is decomposed into a negation operator and an existential quantifier, so that a third scope-bearing element, in this case the necessity operator, can 'intervene.'

The decomposition of the negative quantifier *no* into the negation operator and the existential quantifier has also been proposed by Potts (2000; 2001). The data offered by Potts (2000) closely resemble those by Kratzer (1995). In particular, Potts (2000) observes that the English example in (34) allows the reading paraphrased in (35), where the contribution of *no* is split into the negation operator and the existential quantifier.

(34)   The company need fire no employees.

(35)   It is not the case that the company is obligated to fire any employees.

Evidence in favor of decomposing the quantifier *no* into negation and an existential quantifier is also suggested by an unrelated phenomenon, discussed by Potts (2001). Consider the following sentences:

(36)   a.   Alger was not, as John believed, a spy.
         b.   Alger, as John believed, was not a spy.

The sentence in (36)a is compatible with any belief by John about Alger. In other words, (36)a is felicitous regardless of whether John believed that Alger was a spy or not. By contrast, (36)b is only compatible with John's belief that Alger was *not* a spy. As Potts (2001; p. 55) puts it: "the descriptive generalization is clear: the *As*-clause must follow its negation in order to ignore it." With this descriptive generalization in mind, we can now turn to the sentence below:

(37)   No student was a spy.

As we observed, truth conditions alone do not seem to allow us to distinguish between the two possible representations in (38).

(38)   a. $\forall x \,(student(x) \rightarrow \neg spy(x))$
         b. $\neg \exists x \,(student(x) \,\&\, spy(x))$

Once we consider the descriptive generalization proposed by Potts, however, we can use the correlation between ambiguity of the parenthetical and the structural relationship between negation and the parenthetical itself. Thus, the relevant example is the following:

(39)   No student, as John believed, was a spy

The logic is simple. *As*-parentheticals cannot ignore following negations. Thus, if the parenthetical in (39) can ignore negation (i.e., John believed that every student was indeed a spy), it means that negation occurs before the parenthetical. This is indeed the case. (39) is consistent with a scenario where John believes that all students are spies. Thus, we would conclude, (38)b constitutes the correct representation of the English sentence in (37).

Taking stock, linguistic theory suggests that negative quantifiers should be decomposed into negation and an existential quantifier. Against this background, children's tendency to rephrase the quantified expression *None of the Ns* with a universal quantifier and negation is surprising. One possibility is that children's use of the universal quantifier only reflects a preference to use negation at the level of the verb phrase. A second possibility is that children's preference for paraphrases containing a universal quantifier and negation follows from a different representation of the quantifier under consideration. On this view, children would be expected to differ from adults in their ability to access any interpretation that depends on the representation of *no* as an existential quantifier in the scope of negation. Thus, two interesting questions that we must leave for future research are (a) whether the decomposition of negative quantifiers is subject to any form of cross-linguistic variation and (b) whether children and adults pattern in the same way with respect to the phenomena discussed by Kratzer (1995) or Potts (2000; 2001).

To recap, this section described the design and the results of an experiment investigating children's knowledge of one of the logical properties of downward entailing expressions. The findings indicate that English-speaking children, like adults, interpret sentences containing disjunction in the nuclear scope of the quantificational expression *None of the Ns*, a downward entailing environment, in accordance with the logical properties of downward entailment. Children occasionally differed from adults, however, in their responses. Nevertheless, the differences between children and adults did not conform to the pattern expected by the Conservative Learning model.

2.4 Conclusion

In this chapter we have reviewed previous studies on children's knowledge of phenomena related to entailment relations. In addition, we have reported the findings of an experiment designed to augment previous research by investigating children's interpretation of the disjunction operator *or* in the nuclear scope of the quantificational expression *None of the Ns*, a downward entailing environment. The results of the experiment corroborate the findings from previous research, showing that children's knowledge of downward entailment extends beyond the production and the interpretation of negative polarity items. In particular, children's knowledge of downward entailment includes the logical consequences of downward entailment, an arguably less visible consequence of downward entailment.

It is probably too early to use these data to evaluate the alternative models of language acquisition described in Chapter 1. For one thing, one would like to be able to draw from a larger empirical base before attempting to reach any conclusion about the language acquisition process. It would be wrong to dismiss the phenomena illustrated in this chapter as irrelevant, however. First, the findings show that children as young as 3;10 behave like adults with respect to judgments that depend on the meaning of *None of the Ns* and on the meaning of *or*. The reader might not find children's knowledge of the meaning of *None of the Ns* to be surprising at all. We will not dwell on this issue here, although, as we will see in Chapter 4, the acquisition literature is replete with claims about children's inaccurate knowledge of other quantified expressions. Children's interpretation of *or* must be different, however. Even the most optimistic reader should be surprised by the fact that young children consistently interpret disjunction as inclusive-*or*, a prerequisite for the responses we have observed, despite the fact that the interpretation of disjunction is often consistent with exclusive-*or* in spoken language (see Crain, Gualmini and Pietroski, 2003).[15]

A second consideration has to do with the possible explanation of the pattern under consideration. When we introduced the interpretation of disjunction in the scope of DE operators, we mentioned the analogy between

---

15 Strictly speaking, to show that children are accessing the inclusive-*or* interpretation of disjunction one would also have to consider a context that makes both disjuncts false. An experiment investigating such a context is reported in Gualmini (2001).

natural languages and De Morgan's laws. This does not explain the facts, however. In particular, mentioning De Morgan's laws obscures the fact that negation is only one of the environments in which disjunction receives a conjunctive interpretation. More importantly, the reference to the relevant De Morgan's law does not offer any insight as to *why* the disjunction operator *or* receives the particular interpretation that it receives. A more promising strategy would be to bear in mind that a statement containing the disjunction operator *or* is true in a set of circumstances that corresponds to the union of the sets of circumstances in which each disjunct is true. Thus, one can view the set of circumstances in which only one of the two disjuncts is true as a subset of the set in which the coordinated phrase is true. Put this way, the pattern of entailment we have been looking at does not look too dissimilar from simple entailments from a set to its subsets, the defining property of downward entailment. By inference, one could view the data reported here as showing children's indirect knowledge of notions like set, subset and set-theoretic inclusion.[16]

The findings are also relevant for one of the mechanisms proposed by the Conservative Learning model. As we illustrated in Chapter 1, according to the Conservative Learning model proposed by Tomasello (2000) children can go minimally beyond the input. For example, children can freely substitute nominals in the utterances they are exposed to. The findings suggest that children's competence must be, at the very least, deeper than that. In fact, the findings suggest that, although a syntax-blind mechanism like noun substitution could describe how children come to produce sentences like (40), something more elaborate has to be said to explain how children *interpret* those sentences.

(40)   a.   None of the pirates found a jewel or a necklace.
        b.   Every pirate found a jewel or a necklace.

If noun substitution is all there is to children's ability to go beyond the input, the differences (in the pattern of entailment) between (40)a and (40)b would be totally mysterious.

Finally, the results reported in this chapter show that we can use the Truth Value Judgment task to determine whether or not a given environment is downward entailing for children. At the end of last chapter, we considered various scenarios. In particular, we did not exclude the possibility that children

---

16 As immediate consequence, this line of reasoning casts doubt on recent studies on children's knowledge of quantification according to which children experience difficulty with set-relational quantifiers (see Hurewitz, Gleitman and Gelman, 2002).

would interpret the disjunction operator *or* in downward entailing environments differently from adults. English-speaking four-year-olds do not show this behavior, though. The interpretation of disjunction as assessed in a Truth Value Judgment task thus becomes a useful diagnostic for further research. In particular, once we assume that children can interpret the disjunction operator *or* in accordance with the semantic property of downward entailment, one can investigate the extent to which they do so in other environments that are relevant from the viewpoint of linguistic theory.

CHAPTER 3

The Structure of Child Language

A recurring phenomenon in discussions of the poverty of the stimulus argument is the relevance of linguistic structure in language production and interpretation. As a consequence, the role of linguistic structure has also been the focus of studies of language acquisition. In this chapter we look at structure dependence as it pertains to downward entailment. We start by reviewing previous studies investigating children's adherence to structure dependent principles. Some of these studies concentrate on (the role of structure in) language production in young children. Important as they may be, these studies are vitiated by the usual possible confound; children's productions only provide us with an estimate of the forms (or meanings) licensed by children's grammars, but they do not allow us to draw inferences about what forms or meanings are not licensed by their grammars. In order to sidestep this potential confound, we turn to studies investigating children's comprehension. Finally, we turn to downward entailment. The investigation of downward entailment expands our understanding of children's use of structure dependent notions, thereby allowing us to address one feature of the poverty of the stimulus argument, namely the pervasiveness of structural notions like c-command in language interpretation.

3.1 Structural Constraints on Form

One of the clearest examples of structure dependence of linguistic principles deals with question formation. This phenomenon is often presented by Chomsky to discuss the extent to which the primary linguistic data allow the child to form the correct generalization (see Chomsky, 1971; 1980b and discussion in Piattelli-Palmarini, 1980). Consider the declarative sentence in (1) and the corresponding question in (2).

(1)   The boy is hungry.

(2)   Is the boy hungry?

Let us consider how the child could learn how to ask questions in English. One possibility is that the child comes up with the following rule:

(3)   To form a question, move the first occurrence of *is* from the corresponding declarative form to the beginning of that sentence.

This rule would lead the child to ask the correct question in (2), without having to draw upon any innate language-specific notion. An immediate problem with the rule in (3) is that it could not be used to ask the question corresponding to (4), not to mention (5).

(4)   The boy was hungry.

(5)   The boy ate a lot of food.

The sentences in (4) and (5) only highlight the most visible problem for the hypothesis in (3), namely the fact that it can only be applied to sentences containing the auxiliary *is*. In other words, (3) can only be used in a limited set of cases. The most serious problem lies elsewhere, however. Consider:

(6)   The boy who is sitting on the rug is hungry.

Moving the first occurrence of *is* would yield the ungrammatical question in (7), whereas the correct question is (8).

(7)   *Is the boy who on the rug is hungry?

(8)   Is the boy who is on the rug hungry?

Now, suppose the child modified her initial hypothesis and came up with the following rule:

(9)   To form a question, move the last occurrence of *is* from the corresponding declarative form to the beginning of that sentence.

Then, the child would make mistakes when asking the question corresponding to (10).

(10)   The boy is sitting on the couch that is being vacuumed by the mother.

In fact, the rule in (9) generates (11) as the question counter-part for (10), whereas the correct question is (12).

(11)   *Is the boy is sitting on the couch that being vacuumed by the mother?

(12)   Is the boy sitting on the couch that is being vacuumed by the mother?

This simple set of examples suggests that a structure-blind rule is unlikely to allow the child to converge on the adult grammar in absence of negative evidence. If children follow a rule that only makes reference to structure independent notions, such as the position of a linguistic expression with respect to other words in the sentence, then children should go through a stage during which they produce questions like (7) or (11). By contrast, if children never assume that structure independent notions play any role in language production, these mistakes should not occur. One does not need to turn to the laboratory to see the implausibility of the first scenario; after all, if all children followed a structure independent hypothesis, some of them might continue to do so into adulthood. Nevertheless, some experimental data would be reassuring.

The role of structure dependence in question formation was investigated by Crain and Nakayama (1987). These researchers conducted an Elicited Production task to evoke questions corresponding to sentences containing more than one auxiliary, as in (13).

(13)   The man who is beating the donkey is mean.

In one experimental trial, children were shown a picture depicting one man who was beating his donkey and a second man who was not beating his donkey. Then the child was invited to ask the puppet, Jabba the Hutt, if "the man who is beating the donkey is mean." The purpose of the experiment was to see whether children would ever ask questions like (14), or if they would only ask (15).

(14)   *Is the man who beating the donkey is mean?

(15)   Is the man who is beating the donkey mean?

Children's responses did not allow the experimenter to draw any conclusion, however. Despite the fact that no child ever produced a question like (14), several of the youngest children did produce non-adult questions, such as the following.

(16)   *Is the man who is beating the donkey is mean?

Questions like (16) are ungrammatical in adult English, but they are not necessarily the result of a structure independent rule. Thus, questions like (16) did not readily allow Crain and Nakayama to discriminate whether children followed a structure dependent rule or a structure independent one.[1] In fact, by looking at (16), one cannot tell which occurrence of the auxiliary has been 'copied' by children in the initial position.

To overcome this difficulty, a second experiment was conducted. Children's elicited questions were modeled on target sentences containing an auxiliary and a modal (e.g., "Ask Jabba if the boy who is happy can see Mickey Mouse"). This maneuver did not eliminate children's production of questions containing a copy of the targeted element, but the results do suggest that children were not adopting a structure independent hypothesis in deciding which verb should be moved or copied. Children always moved or copied the verb occurring in the main clause. In other words, children produced ungrammatical questions like (17), alongside the grammatical question in (18).

(17)   *Can the boy who is happy can see Mickey Mouse?

(18)   Can the boy who is happy see Mickey Mouse?

However, questions like the following, in which the moved (or copied) auxiliary starts from within the relative clause, were unattested in children's productions.

(19)   *Is the boy who happy can see Mickey Mouse?

(20)   *Is the boy who is happy can see Mickey Mouse?

To recap, children's questions elicited by Crain and Nakayama (1987) are not fully adult-like. Some children asked questions differing in form from those

---

1 See also Nakayama (1987).

licensed by the adult grammar. These questions did not differ from the adult grammar in the way predicted by a structure independent hypothesis, however. This fact becomes even more noteworthy in light of the attested mistakes. Children apparently can deviate from the adult grammar. Nevertheless, their productions yield a pattern that can only be accounted for by a structure dependent hypothesis, something that Chomsky (1980b; p. 40) anticipated in the following passage: "Children make many errors in language learning, but none such as [(14) – *AG*], prior to appropriate training or evidence."

The relevance of the Crain and Nakayama findings has been recently challenged by two different groups of researchers.[2] Pullum and Scholz (2002) have argued that the findings are not as surprising as assumed by Crain and Nakayama (1987), because the assumption that children cannot rely on any relevant input is flawed. In particular, according to Pullum and Scholz (2002), it is unwarranted to assume that questions containing two auxiliaries are absent from the primary linguistic data. By contrast, Lewis and Elman (2002) have argued that these experimental findings are not as surprising as assumed by Crain and Nakayama (1987), because the assumption that children should hear questions containing two auxiliaries in order to form the correct rule is flawed. Let us consider each challenge in turn.

As we discussed in Chapter 1, Pullum and Scholz (2002) discuss one assumption that underlies much research in language acquisition, namely the assumption that the input is impoverished. Discussing question formation, Pullum and Scholz (2002) start from the following statement by Chomsky (1980b; p. 40).

---

2 Sampson (2002; pp. 89-90) suggests that if he had participated in the Crain and Nakayama experiment, he would have resorted to questions like *The man who is beating the donkey is mean, isn't he?* or *Is he mean, the man who is beating the donkey?* Since Crain and Nakayama do not report any questions of this kind, Sampson (2002; p. 90) hypothesizes that "whatever the subjects were doing, they were not asking questions in the way that was most natural for them. Apparently the experimental situation must have involved an element of training the children in literary question-formation." We cannot address this type of criticism in absence of a more explicit proposal as to what could constitute the element of training hypothesized by Sampson (2002). However, it is worth pointing out that children did indeed produce sentences similar to the ones considered by Sampson (2000). Such sentences have not been discussed in following literature because they do not discriminate whether children follow a structure dependent or a structure independent rule.

"A person might go through much or all of his life without ever having been exposed to relevant evidence, but he will nevertheless unerringly employ [a structure dependent rule - *AG*], never [a structure independent rule - *AG*]."

Although much research has endorsed the validity of the assumption underlying Chomsky's reasoning, Pullum and Scholz (2002) argue that such an assumption is blatantly fallacious. In particular, Pullum and Scholz (2002) maintain that children could find abundant examples in the primary linguistic data that would allow them to reject a structure independent hypothesis in favor of the correct structure dependent rule. In support of their claim, they offer various examples of questions containing more than one auxiliary from different databases, including the Wall Street Journal. Some examples from Pullum and Scholz (2002; pp. 42-43) are reported below:

(21)   a.   Is a young professional who lives in a bachelor condo as much
                a part of the middle class as a family in the suburbs?
        b.   Is what I'm doing in the shareholders' best interest?

In response to Fodor and Crowther's (2002) concern about the 'exotic' nature of such examples, Scholz and Pullum (2002; p. 9) offer an even simpler case:

(22)   Is what's left mine?

We believe that Pullum and Scholz's observations miss the mark. First, Pullum and Scholz (2002) seem to assume that the task faced by the child is to learn that the question in (23) is grammatical.

(23)   Is the boy who is sitting on the rug hungry?

As pointed out by Lasnik and Uriagereka (2002), however, this is the easiest, and possibly the least interesting, fraction of the child's task. Not only must the child learn that (23) is a grammatical question, the child must also learn that (24) is *not* a grammatical question of English.[3]

---

3 A logical possibility would be that children do not produce questions like (24) because they have never heard those questions. This is the scenario predicted by the Conservative Learning model proposed by Tomasello (2000). As we discussed in Chapter 1, however, it is incumbent on this view to explain how children eventually converge on some generalization that allows them to produce (and interpret) sentences that they have

(24)   *Is the boy who sitting on the rug is hungry?

If Pullum and Scholz (2002) want to argue that the input is less impoverished than usually assumed, they should show where, other than in linguistics textbooks, the child can find evidence of the ungrammaticality of (24). The *relevant* information is what the asterisk in (24) stands for. Showing that child directed speech contains questions like (22) has very little relevance. If child directed speech has to provide the child with evidence that questions like (24) are ungrammatical, then the child's only chance of success involves asking a question like (25) hoping that his authoritative Soprano-style father will reply as in (26).

(25)   *Are all the cannolis that left are for me?

(26)   Watch your mouth kiddo! We don't talk like that around the table! You say 'are all the cannolis that are left for me?'.

In the absence of this kind of input, the examples offered by Pullum and Scholz (2002) can only lead the child to conclude that (23) is *one* possible way to ask the question corresponding to the declarative sentence *The boy who is sitting on the rug is hungry*, but those examples do not necessarily rule out (24) as another possible way of asking the same question. At most, the examples offered by Pullum and Scholz (2002) will lead the child to modify her hypothesis as follows:

(27)   To form a question, move any occurrence of *is* from the corresponding declarative form to the beginning of that sentence.

As we mentioned in Chapter 1, Pullum and Scholz might have in mind some form of Uniqueness Constraint that only allows children to reserve *one form* for each intended meaning. It is not clear to what extent this mechanism would allow children to converge on the correct grammar, however.[4] Although it might

---

never encountered before. Moreover, on this view it would be difficult to explain why the children interviewed by Crain and Nakayama repeated a 'copy' of the auxiliary verb. Presumably, those children never encountered those sentences in the primary linguistic data.

4 See also Fodor and Crain (1987).

be true that different forms are always accompanied by subtle differences in meaning, for most conversational situations one can find more than one form that would do the job. For example, all the following questions adapted from Sampson (2002) are well-formed, and it is difficult to find a context in which only one question would be appropriate.

(28)   a.   Is the boy who is sitting on the rug hungry?
        b.   The boy who is sitting on the rug, is he hungry?
        c.   The boy who is sitting on the rug is hungry. Isn't he?

Similar problems for the uniqueness constraint arise, once we turn to language comprehension. In this case, the uniqueness constraint would only allow a given form to express *one* meaning. Thus, children would never be able to assign multiple meanings to the same form. On this scenario, the pervasiveness of ambiguity in natural languages would look mysterious.

A second shortcoming of the Pullum and Scholz proposal is discussed by Crain and Pietroski (2002). These researchers point out that structure dependence is a general constraint on all principles of the grammar. For purposes of the argument, let us concede that children learn how structure dependence plays a role in question formation in the way proposed by Pullum and Scholz (2002). The child's task would be far from complete, since structure dependence plays a role in many linguistic phenomena other than question formation. If we assume that some evidence must be available to children for each and every one of these phenomena, the prediction would be that there should be stages of language development at which children have mastered how structure dependence plays a role with respect to *one* phenomenon, but not necessarily for others. Thus, even if children somehow manage to expunge any structure independent rule for question formation from their grammar, they would have to go through the same 'unlearning' process for all the phenomena for which structure dependence plays a role. We will return to this issue at the end of the chapter, after we discuss the role of structure dependence in children's knowledge of downward entailment.

Let us now turn to the study by Lewis and Elman (2002). These researchers constructed a simple recurrent network to model question formation in English (see Elman, 1990 for a discussion of simple recurrent networks). The network was trained through a three-stage training process with degree of complexity increasing at each stage. Importantly, the network was presented with *yes/no* questions (e.g., "Is the big dog in the car scary?"), but it was not presented with any questions containing two auxiliaries (i.e., questions like "Is the farmer who is beating the donkey mean?"). Despite the lack of questions containing two auxiliaries, Lewis and Elman (2002; p. 364) argue that "the network does not make the predictions corresponding to the ungrammatical [question – *AG*] – *i.e.*, the network does not predict [a gerund – *AG*] following '*who*'." In other words, the network consistently predicts that a substring like (29) should be followed by an auxiliary.

(29)   Is the boy who ____

In addition, Lewis and Elman (2002) observe that if the network is *presented* with a substring that contains an auxiliary following *who* as in (30), the network predicts the occurrence of a third auxiliary, thereby predicting the kind of ungrammatical questions that children produced in the Crain and Nakayama study.

(30)   Is the boy who is smoking ____

In short, Lewis and Elman (2002; pp. 368-9) observe that "the most prominent and persistent of the errors is the prediction of an auxiliary following the participle, i.e., '*is the boy who is smoking is*'" and argue that this correctly models children's ungrammatical questions reported by Crain and Nakayama.

We wish to raise some concerns with the Lewis and Elman study. First, it is hard to understand what the network really learned. From what one can gather, we could simply say that the network has learned that a sequence like *who smoking* is unacceptable whereas *who is smoking* is acceptable. This might be an epiphenomenon of structure dependence in English, but it is not the same thing as structure dependence. In fact, one wonders if the same network could predict a question like (31), which is well formed despite the presence of the sequence *who smoking*.[5]

(31)   Is the boy who smoking offends still here?

Similarly, one wonders what the network would do with a question like (32), which is ungrammatical, despite the fact that each pair of consecutive words can occur in a grammatical question.

---

5 The question in (31) could be uttered in a context in which it is known that there are two boys, one of whom becomes upset if someone is smoking.

(32)   *Is the boy who is smoking offends still here?

Second, Lewis and Elman's claim that the network models children's mistakes documented by Crain and Nakayama (1987) is misleading. Sentences containing three occurrences of *is* were indeed collected by Crain and Nakayama (1987). But these researchers concluded that those forms could not be used to distinguish between the application of a structure dependent rule and the application of a structure independent one. Accordingly, Crain and Nakayama (1987) modified the experimental protocol in order to elicit questions containing an auxiliary and a modal. Parsimony suggests that the same maneuver should have been implemented by Lewis and Elman (2002). For example, Lewis and Elman should investigate whether the network predicts the occurrence of an auxiliary or a modal following the substring below.

(33)   Can the boy who is smoking ___

Third, even if we assume that the interpretation advanced by Lewis and Elman is correct, their account still faces one of the problems encountered by Pullum and Scholz. Assuming that the results documented by Lewis and Elman show that a neural network can model question formation, they do not show that the network has converged on a structure dependent notion that would also be relevant for other linguistic phenomena. If structure dependence is at issue, one must show that the *same network* (after undergoing the same training) would make the correct prediction once we turn to other linguistic phenomena where structure dependence plays a role. After all, there seems to be no empirical evidence suggesting that children's use of structure dependence is construction specific. In other words, there is no empirical evidence suggesting that children acquire the importance of structure dependence for question formation without also acquiring that structure dependence plays a role for other phenomena of natural languages (see below).

To recap, we have reviewed one study showing children's adherence to structure dependent principles in question formation. We have also discussed two accounts of question formation in children that do not posit any innate structure dependent principles and we have argued that both accounts face considerable theoretical and empirical difficulties. To further strengthen our argument, we now turn to more experimental studies showing that children's adherence to structure dependent principles extends beyond question formation. These studies focus on language comprehension.

3.2 Structural Constraints on Interpretation

The first experimental investigation of children's adherence to the structure dependent notion of c-command in language interpretation dealt with the Binding Theory. Consider the examples in (34). The pronoun *he* cannot be referentially dependent on the referring expression, *the Ninja Turtle*, in (34)a. By contrast, co-reference is possible in (34)b.

(34)   a.   He said the Ninja Turtle has the best smile.
        b.   As he was leaving, the Ninja Turtle smiled.

One standard explanation for the prohibition against referential dependence in (34)a is that a pronoun cannot be referentially dependent on a referring expression that it c-commands (see Reinhart, 1976)[6]. In (34)b, the pronoun does not c-command the NP *the Ninja Turtle*, so co-reference is permitted.

Given the adult pattern and the structural notion that explains such a pattern, the empirical question is whether children follow the same principles as adults do. To address this question, Crain and McKee (1985) developed a new experimental technique, the Truth Value Judgment task. As we saw, the Truth Value Judgment task is an experimental technique that allows the experimenter to determine whether the child's grammar licenses a particular interpretation for a given grammatical construction. In the particular case at hand, Crain and McKee (1985) sought to determine whether children know that the sentence in (35) is ambiguous, allowing both a co-referential and a deictic reading, whereas (36) is unambiguous and only allows a deictic reading of the pronoun *he*.

(35)   When he stole the chickens, the lion was in the box.

(36)   He ate the hamburger when the Smurf was in the fence.

The finding was that even two to three year olds would consistently reject co-reference between the pronoun *he* and the NP *the Smurf* in the case of (36), but they would accept co-reference between *he* and *the lion* in the case of (35).

---

6 Recall the definition of c-command: A c-commands B if and only if (i) the first branching node dominating A also dominates B, (ii) A does not dominate B and (iii) A is different from B (see Reinhart, 1976; Chomsky, 1981).

Thus, the experimental findings suggest that the constraint on co-reference operative in child grammar distinguishes between (35) and (36), despite the fact that the linear order between the pronoun and the noun phrase is the same. By inference, the constraint on co-reference endorsed by children must make reference to an abstract representation of (35) and (36) that makes available two different relationships between the pronoun and the referential expression in those sentences, e.g., c-command.

The role of c-command can also be observed in the interpretation of pronouns that appear in *wh*-questions. For example, we can consider the so-called strong crossover phenomenon (see Postal, 1971).

(37)   Who said he has the best smile?

The question in (37) can be interpreted as a question about which individual said that some specific male available in the context has the best smile. This is the deictic reading represented in (38)a. In addition, the question in (37) can be interpreted as a question about which male individual claimed to have the best smile. This is the bound reading paraphrased in (38)b.

(38)   a.   <u>who</u> said he has the best smile   (Deictic reading)
        b.   <u>who</u> said <u>he</u> has the best smile   (Bound pronoun reading)

Let us now turn to (39).

(39)   Who did he say has the best smile?

The question in (39) is unambiguous. In particular, (39) can only be interpreted as a question asking which individuals attributed to some other salient male individual the property of having the best smile (i.e., the deictic reading), and it cannot be asking which male individual claimed to have to best smile (i.e., the bound pronoun reading). The structural notion of c-command has been invoked to explain the absence of the bound pronoun reading in strong crossover questions like (39). Chomsky (1981) proposed that the question in (39) is derived through movement of the *wh*-word *who* from the trace position indicated below.

(40)   who did he say   t   has the best smile.

In the course of the derivation, the *wh*-word *who* 'crosses over' the pronoun *he* on its way to its surface position, leaving behind a 'trace' in its original position, as in (40). Chomsky (1981) proposed that traces of *wh*-movement cannot be referentially dependent on expressions that c-command them; in this respect, traces are like referential expressions, as in (34)a.

Turning to child language, the question is whether children know that (39) is unambiguous whereas (37) is ambiguous. Empirical evidence that children know the relevant linguistic principles by age three comes from a Truth Value Judgment task conducted by Crain and Thornton (1998). These researchers tested children's knowledge of strong crossover by considering their interpretation of sentences like (41) and (42).

(41)   I know who he said has the best food. Grover and Yogi Bear.

(42)   I know who said he has the best food. Grover and Yogi Bear.

The experimental findings show that children distinguish between (41) and (42). In particular, children as young as 3:7 interpret (41) as meaning that some male character available in the context, but different from Grover or Yogi Bear, said that Yogi Bear and Grover had the best food (i.e., the deictic interpretation). By contrast, children can interpret (42) as meaning that Grover and Yogi Bear claimed to have the best food (i.e., the bound pronoun interpretation).

Taking stock, experimental investigations of child language show that children's use of structure dependent rules extends beyond language production. Furthermore, children seem to make use of structure dependent principles across a variety of phenomena instantiated in the target grammar that share little resemblance at the superficial level.

The role of c-command has also been investigated in cases of apparent mismatches between children and adults. For example, Lidz and Musolino (2002) investigated the role of the structural notion of c-command in children's resolution of scopal ambiguity. Consider the examples in (43).

(43)   The Smurf didn't catch two birds.

The example in (43) is ambiguous. On one interpretation, it can be paraphrased as meaning that it is not true that the Smurf caught two birds. On this interpretation, negation takes scope over the quantifier *two*. This corresponds to an *isomorphic* interpretation since the scope relation between negation and *two birds* can be directly read off their surface syntactic position. Alternatively, (43) can be interpreted as meaning that there are two birds that the Smurf did not catch. On this interpretation, the quantified noun phrase *two birds* takes scope over negation. This interpretation can be described as a *non-isomorphic* interpretation, because the scope relation between the two scope-bearing expressions is the reverse of the one given by their surface syntactic position.

The main finding emerging from child language research is that young children, unlike adults, display a strong preference for the isomorphic interpretation of sentences like (43).[7] Accordingly, this phenomenon was described as the Observation of Isomorphism by Musolino (1998). An interesting question raised by the Observation of Isomorphism is whether children's preference for the isomorphic interpretation of quantified sentences reflects a preference for the scope relations dictated by the linear order or a preference for the scope relations dictated by the structural relationship between the relevant operators. If we only focus on English, it is not possible to address this issue, since negation both precedes and c-commands the noun phrase *two birds* in (43). For this reason, Lidz and Musolino (2002) decided to investigate the interpretation of scopally ambiguous sentences by children who were in the process of learning Kannada, a Dravidian language spoken in south-western India. In Kannada, in contrast to English, linear order and structural dominance can be teased apart. In particular, the basic word order of Kannada is SOV with negation following the verb and the object noun phrase, but the structural relations are the same as English, with negation c-commanding the verb and the object noun phrase. The experimental findings collected by Lidz and Musolino (2002) show that English- and Kannada-speaking 4-year-olds equally interpret sentences like (43) assigning wide scope to negation. Now, since negation and the indefinite noun phrase occur with opposite orders in English and Kannada, linear precedence does not explain the uniformity of children's responses. The conclusion reached by Lidz and Musolino (2002) is that, in assigning wide

---

7 The Observation of Isomorphism proposed by Musolino (1998) and Musolino, Crain and Thornton (2000) is intended to describe a wider range of facts about children's interpretation of quantified sentences, some of which have been introduced in Chapter 2. We will engage in a more detailed investigation of scope resolution in child language in Chapter 5.

scope to negation, children exposed to either language follow some structural relation that is shared by both English and Kannada.

It is important to put the Lidz and Musolino study in perspective. The Lidz and Musolino study does not pertain to a principle of UG in the way that the other studies reviewed above do. For present purposes, we can observe that the study simply pertains to whatever factor is responsible for children's non-adult preference for isomorphic interpretations in English. That said, the importance of the Lidz and Musolino study lies in the fact that these authors showed that one feature of UG, namely structure dependence, can even be observed by looking at one phenomenon where children *differ* from adults. Children differ from adults in how they interpret scopally ambiguous sentences like (43), but they only differ from adults in limited ways. In particular, they do not differ from adults to the extent of violating the structure dependent character of natural languages.

A further investigation of children's adherence to structure dependence deals with the semantic property of downward entailment. The next section recalls the relevant facts from Chapter 1 and reviews a relevant investigation in more detail.

3.3 Structure Dependence and Polarity Phenomena

The semantic property of downward entailment was introduced in Chapter 2. In discussing the consequences of downward entailment, we also mentioned the relevance of the structural notion of c-command. Roughly, we observed that c-command constrains the domain of downward entailing operators. Consider the examples from (44) through (46). Example (44) shows that negation only licenses inferences from a set to its subsets in its c-command domain; the same contrast holds for the licensing of NPIs, as shown in (45), and whether or not the disjunction operator is assigned the conjunctive interpretation as shown in (46).

(44)   a.   The boy who majored in linguistics did not learn <u>a Romance language</u>

         $\Rightarrow$ The boy who majored in linguistics did not learn <u>French</u>.

   b.   The boy who did not major in linguistics learned <u>a Romance language</u>

         *$\Rightarrow$ The boy who did not major in linguistics learned <u>French</u>.

(45)   a.   The boy who majored in linguistics did not learn <u>any</u>
                  Romance language.
       b.   *The boy who did not major in linguistics learned <u>any</u>
                  Romance language.

(46)   a.   The boy who majored in linguistics did not learn French <u>or</u>
                  Spanish
                         ⇒   The boy who majored in linguistics did not
                                learn French <u>and</u> the boy who majored in
                                linguistics did not learn Spanish.
       b.   The boy who did not major in linguistics learned French or
                  Spanish
                         *⇒   The boy who did not major in linguistics
                                learned French <u>and</u> the boy who did not
                                major in linguistics learned Spanish.

The role of c-command in constraining children's assignment of the
conjunctive interpretation to sentences containing the disjunction operator *or*
was investigated by Crain, Gardner, Gualmini and Rabbin (2002). Drawing
upon the experimental design of Experiment I illustrated in Chapter 2, Crain et
al. (2002) investigated whether the structure dependent notion of c-command
constrains downward entailment in child language. These researchers used the
pattern in (46) to determine whether children know that linear precedence is not
sufficient to license the conjunctive interpretation of disjunction; the licensing
operator must c-command disjunction.

A Truth Value Judgment task was designed to determine if children know
that the disjunction operator *or* receives a conjunctive interpretation when it is c-
commanded by negation as in (46)a, but not when it is merely preceded by
negation as in (46)b. The experiment employed the Prediction Mode (see
Chierchia et al., 1998).[8] Thirty children ranging in age between 3;11 and 5;9
(mean age: 5;0) participated in the experiment, divided in two groups. These
children were presented with two sentences in which negation c-commanded the

---

8 This choice was dictated by the desire to avoid the infelicity of using the scalar
term *or* in a context that warranted the computation of Scalar Implicatures (see our
review of Boster and Crain, 1993 in Chapter 2).

disjunction operator *or* (as in (46)a) and two sentences in which negation preceded but did not c-command the disjunction operator *or* (as in (46)b).[9]

In one of the trials of the Crain et al. study, children were told a story about two girls who had lost a tooth. The girls knew that the Tooth Fairy would come during the night and would give them a reward in exchange for their lost tooth. One girl decided to go to bed right away, while the other girl decided to stay up late to see what the Tooth Fairy looked like. Then, the Tooth Fairy arrived, with two jewels and two dimes. At this point, the story was interrupted so that the puppet, Merlin the Magician, could make a prediction about what would happen in the remainder of the story. One group of children heard (47), in which negation both precedes and c-commands the disjunction operator *or*, while the second group heard (48), in which negation precedes but does not c-command *or*.

(47)   The girl who stayed up late will <u>not</u> get a dime <u>or</u> a jewel.

(48)   The girl who <u>didn't</u> go to sleep will get a dime <u>or</u> a jewel.

At this point, the telling of the story resumed. As events ensued, the Tooth Fairy gave a dime and a jewel to the girl that was sleeping, but the Tooth Fairy was disappointed to see that the other girl was still awake. The little girl explained that she had decided to stay up to see what the Tooth Fairy looked like. At the end, the Tooth Fairy decided to give a jewel, but not a dime, to the girl that had stayed up late. Following the completion of the story, Merlin reminded the child subjects of his prediction:

(49)   I said that the girl who stayed up late would <u>not</u> get a dime <u>or</u> a jewel.

(50)   I said that the girl who <u>didn't</u> go to sleep would get a dime <u>or</u> a jewel.

Because of the interaction between downward entailment and c-command, the two sentences generate different entailment patterns. In particular, only (49) licenses the conjunctive interpretation and requires that the girl under

---

9 The two groups were presented with the same stories. However, the first group heard a sentence in which negation preceded and c-commanded the disjunction operator *or* as a description for the first two trials, while the second group heard a sentence in which negation simply preceded, but did not c-command, the disjunction operator *or* for the same trials. The remaining two trials were presented in the opposite fashion.

consideration did not get a dime and that she did not get a jewel. By contrast, (50) is true in a wider range of circumstances: (a) if the girl under consideration got a dime but no jewel, (b) if she got a jewel but no dime; and probably even (c) if she got both.

The experimental hypothesis was that children would reject sentences like (49), but would accept ones like (50). The results confirmed this hypothesis. Children rejected sentences like (49) 92% of the time whereas they accepted sentences like (50) 87% of the time. The findings indicate that children distinguish between the entailment patterns associated with *or* in the two sentences. In particular, children know that (49) requires both disjuncts to be true (i.e., the girl should not receive a jewel and she should not receive a dime), whereas (50) only requires one of the two disjuncts to be true (i.e., the girl should receive at least one of the two objects).

It is time to take stock. The findings documented by Crain et al. (2002) show that linear precedence is not a sufficient condition to establish a downward entailing environment. If linear precedence was a sufficient condition to establish a downward entailing environment, children should have interpreted (50) incorrectly, according to the inference scheme below.

(51)   I said that the girl who didn't go to sleep would get a dime or a jewel
          *⇒   I said that the girl who didn't go to sleep would get a
                   dime and that the girl who didn't go to sleep would
                   get a jewel.

Since children did not make the inference indicated in (51), Crain et al. (2002) concluded that children (like adults) are guided by the same constraint on the effect of a DE operator, namely c-command.

This being said, we would like to extend the Crain et al. study by addressing a potential confound of that study. Recall the target sentences, repeated below as (52) and (53).

(52)   I said that the girl who stayed up late would not get a dime or a jewel.

(53)   I said that the girl who didn't go to sleep would get a dime or a jewel.

The target sentences differ with respect to the structural relationship between negation and disjunction. This is not the only difference between the two sentences, however. Among other factors, the two sentences differ in the number of words that intervene between negation and disjunction: negation and disjunction are much closer in (52) than they are in (53). Now, if linear precedence is a possible domain general cue that children pay attention to, nothing excludes the possibility that 'distance' could also play a role.[10] To rule out this hypothesis, one has to show that (a) children assign the conjunctive interpretation to (sentences containing) disjunction regardless of how far disjunction is from negation, or that (b) children refrain from assigning the conjunctive interpretation to disjunction if this is merely preceded by negation, even if the two operators are very close to each other. The next section reports the design and the results of two experiments taking up these scenarios, in turn.

Within the present context, the following experiments are relevant for a second reason. In Chapter 2, we presented some empirical evidence showing that English-speaking children, just like adults, assign the conjunctive interpretation to the disjunction *or* when it occurs in the scope of a downward entailing operator. In particular, we reported the findings of an experiment showing that children 'correctly' reject a sentence like (54) in a context in which one of the pirates had found the jewel.

(54)   None of the pirates found the jewel or the necklace.

This was not a trivial finding, because children might have instantiated a different pattern. In any event, the null assumption was that children would have instantiated a pattern that made reference to the same primitives of adult languages. The experiments illustrated in the next section examine this prediction, by considering whether the pattern instantiated by children makes reference to linguistic structure.

3.4 Experimental Design

In order to investigate the role of linear distance in explaining previous findings, we designed two experiments employing the Truth Value Judgment task. In Experiment II, children were presented with sentences in which the disjunction operator *or* was preceded and c-commanded by negation, but these two

---

10 On this matter, it is instructive to observe that the notion of distance, in various forms, is often used to explain psycholinguistic phenomena. Focusing on child language, for example, Chomsky (1969) makes reference to Rosenbaum's (1967) Minimal Distance Principle while commenting on the interpretation of sentences like *John asked Bill to leave* and *John promised Bill to leave*.

operators were further apart from each other than in the Crain et al. study. In Experiment III, children were presented with sentences in which the disjunction operator *or* was preceded but not c-commanded by negation, and these two operators were close to each other. Let us consider each experiment in turn.

3.4.1 Experiment II

This experiment was designed to determine whether children's interpretation of disjunction in the scope of negation was affected by the distance between the two operators. Recall that a possible objection to the conclusion by Crain et al. (2002) was that c-command was confounded with proximity. To address this possible confounding factor, we conducted an experiment in which the structural relations were not altered, but the distance between negation and disjunction was increased. To minimize the differences between the present study and the one by Crain et al. (2002), the experiment employed the Prediction Mode of the Truth Value Judgment task.

Thirty children participated in the experiment. The children ranged in age between 3;08 and 6;05 with a mean age of 4;09. Each child was presented with two target trials, one warm-up and one filler trial. One of the target trials is described below.

(55)   "This is a story about Winnie the Pooh, Eeyore and Arthur. Eeyore is very sad and Winnie the Pooh says "You need something to cheer you up. Let's go to Arthur's. He always has lots of good food!". When they arrive at Arthur's store, Arthur shows them some goodies: a strawberry, a cookie and a cake."

At this point the storyteller would stop and ask Merlin the Magician if he could predict what would happen next. Then, Merlin made the following prediction.

(56)   I predict that Winnie the pooh will not let Eeyore eat the cookie or the cake.

Then the story resumed, as in (57):

(57)   "Winnie the Pooh invites Eeyore to eat the strawberry because it is very healthy but Eeyore says: "Well, I know that the strawberry is very healthy, but I really need something sweet," to which Winnie the Pooh

responds: "Ok, you can have the cookie then, but not the cake, because that's too much sugar for you!".".

Following the completion of the story, Merlin reminded the child of his prediction.

(58)   I said that Winnie the Pooh would not let Eeyore eat the cookie or the cake.

Let us spell out our predictions. Negation precedes and c-commands disjunction in (58). Thus the preferred reading of the target sentence is that Winnie the Pooh would not let Eeyore eat the cookie and he would not let him eat the cake. This interpretation makes the sentence false, because Winnie the Pooh did allow Eeyore to eat the cookie. In short, the conjunctive interpretation of disjunction arises despite the linguistic material intervening between negation and disjunction.

Against this background, if children's behavior documented by Crain et al. (2002) was dictated by the distance between negation and disjunction, children could fail to assign the conjunctive interpretation to the disjunction operator *or* and accept the target sentence. By contrast, if children's interpretation of the target sentence was dictated by the structural relation between *not* and *or*, they should reject it without being thrown off by the distance between those two logical operators. This is exactly what happened. The child subjects rejected the target sentence on 51 out of 60 trials (85%). As controls, a group of 10 undergraduates participated in a videotaped version of the experiment. This control group rejected the target sentences 95% of the time. (See the Appendix for more experimental details).

These findings show that c-command is a sufficient condition for the application of the familiar entailment pattern. When disjunction is c-commanded by a downward entailing operator like negation, children, like adults, apply the relevant De Morgan's law, regardless of the distance between those two logical operators. Moreover, children assigned the conjunctive interpretation to disjunction in our experiment to the same extent as in the Crain et al. (2002) experiment, despite the difference in distance between the two operators in the sentences employed in the two experiments (see (59) and (60)).[11]

---

11 Recall that children in the Crain et al. (2002) study rejected sentences like (60) 92% of the time.

(59)   Winnie the Pooh would <u>not</u> let Eeyore eat the cookie <u>or</u> the cake.

(60)   The girl who stayed up late will <u>not</u> get a dime <u>or</u> a jewel.

Thus, the relative proximity of negation and disjunction is not a necessary condition for the conjunctive interpretation of disjunction. To determine whether it is a *sufficient* condition, we turn to the next experiment.

3.4.2 Experiment III

The present experiment was designed to determine whether children in the Crain et al. study refrained from assigning the conjunctive interpretation to disjunction in sentences in which disjunction is not c-commanded by negation because of the number of words intervening between the two operators. Recall the relevant target sentence from the Crain et al. study.

(61)   The girl who <u>didn't</u> go to sleep will get a dime <u>or</u> a jewel.

Crain et al. report that children didn't assign a conjunctive interpretation to the disjunction operator *or* when interpreting (61), thereby showing that linear precedence by negation alone does not license such an interpretation. As the reader can observe, however, the distance between negation and disjunction in (61) is less than optimal. In particular, the distance between the two logical operators is bigger than that in the target sentences used by Crain et al. (2002) in the c-command condition (see (62)).

(62)   The girl who stayed up late will <u>not</u> get a dime <u>or</u> a jewel.

As we observed, one could hypothesize that children did not assign a conjunctive interpretation to disjunction in (61), because the relevant operators are further apart in (61) than in (62). To investigate this possibility, children were presented with sentences in which negation and disjunction occurred at the same distance as (62), but no c-command relation held between the two operators. As in the Crain et al. (2002) study, the experiment employed the Prediction Mode of the Truth Value Judgment task.

Thirty-five children participated in the experiment. The children ranged in age between 3;05 and 6;05 with a mean age of 4;11. Each child was presented with two target trials, one warm-up and one filler trial. Let us describe one of the target trials.

(63)   "This is a story about a Karate Man and two Pooh Bears, one very big and the other smaller. The Karate Man has just finished his training and is about to eat his after-training snack: some honey, a donut and a strawberry. When the Pooh Bears arrive, the Karate Man starts bragging about how strong he is and says: "I bet I am so strong that I can lift each one of you! In fact, I promise that I will give some of my food to whoever I cannot lift." The Pooh Bears accept the bet and the small Pooh Bear walks in front of the Karate Man. The Karate Man looks at him and easily lifts him. Then, the Karate Man looks at the bigger Pooh Bear and says: "Hmm, this is going to be tough. Maybe I made a mistake. Well, let's see." He tries to lift the big Pooh Bear but he fails. He walks around the Pooh Bear and looks for an easier grip but he fails again. At this point he says: "Well, it looks like I lost my bet with you big Pooh Bear. Now I have to give you some of my food!"."

As in Experiment II, the storyteller stopped at this point of the story to ask Merlin the Magician to guess what would happen next. Below is Merlin's prediction.

(64)   I predict that the Karate Man will give the Pooh Bear he cannot lift the honey or the donut.

Then the story resumed.

(65)   "The Karate Man looks at his food and says: "Maybe, I should give him some honey because I know that's what bears like, but I am sure he already had some honey today. Well, I could give him the donut then, but I will keep the strawberry because that's what makes me strong!" and gives the big Pooh Bear the donut."

At this point, Merlin reminded the child of his prediction, as in (66).

(66)   I predicted that the Karate Man would give the Pooh Bear he could not lift the honey or the donut.

It is important to observe that negation and disjunction appear close to each other in the target sentence. If proximity between negation and disjunction was a sufficient condition for the assignment of a conjunctive interpretation to disjunction, then children should resort to such an interpretation for (66). On this scenario, children should interpret (66) as in (67), and reject the target sentence, on the grounds that the Karate Man had not given the honey to the Pooh Bear that he had not been able to lift.

(67)   I predicted that the Karate Man would give the Pooh Bear he could not lift the honey <u>and</u> that he would give the Pooh Bear he could not lift the donut.

By contrast, if one takes into account the structural relationship between the two operators, the absence of any intervening words is irrelevant. If the conjunctive interpretation of disjunction is assigned only when negation c-commands the disjunction operator, then children should refrain from accessing the conjunctive interpretation of disjunction in (66), just like they did in the Crain et al. study.

This is exactly what happened. The children who participated in the experiment accepted the target sentence on 56 out of 70 trials (80%) (see the Appendix for experimental details). A group of 12 undergraduates participated as controls; they always accepted the target sentences. Thus, children did not assign the conjunctive interpretation to the disjunction operator *or*, despite the proximity between negation and disjunction. Moreover, children refrained from assigning the conjunctive interpretation to the disjunction operator *or* to the same extent for the target sentences of our experiment and for the target sentences used by Crain et al. (2002), despite the fact that the distance between negation and disjunction differs in the two sentences (see (68) and (69)). [12]

(68)   The Karate Man will give the Pooh Bear he could <u>not</u> lift the honey <u>or</u> the donut.

(69)   The girl who <u>didn't</u> go to sleep will get a dime <u>or</u> a jewel.

This shows that proximity between these two operators is not relevant for children's interpretation.

---

12 Recall that children in the Crain et al. (2002) study accepted sentences like (69) 87% of the time.

3.4.3 Summary of the Experimental Findings

We first reviewed the findings of an experiment by Crain et al. (2002). We noted a possible confound in the Crain et al. study that was addressed in two follow-up experiments. These experiments investigated children's knowledge of the interaction between downward entailment and the structure dependent notion of c-command. The experimental results corroborate the findings of previous research, and they resist explanation on accounts that do not attribute knowledge of structure dependent principles to young children.

3.5 Conclusion

The present chapter focused on structure dependence in child language. We first reviewed previous studies showing children's adherence to structure dependent notions across a variety of linguistic phenomena. Each study extended our understanding of structure dependence in child language. Downward entailment was no exception, as it allowed us to consider structure dependence and linear proximity in a case where they met head on. Furthermore, downward entailment allowed us to test children's adherence to structure dependence by considering their interpretation of sentences that do not differ in the possibility of occurring in the child's environment.

It is useful to underscore the role of structural notions like c-command in linguistic research. It may be argued that the argument invoking c-command is not sound, in part because hierarchical configurations that resemble c-command can also be attributed to some non-linguistic entities. For example, Sampson (1997) argued that the manipulation of structured rather than unstructured entities would inevitably provide an advantage to any organism (see also Clark, 2001). We can rephrase the objections by saying that if c-command is not idiosyncratic to language, then it could be learned using the same domain-general learning mechanisms that are used for other non-linguistic phenomena. We think this hypothesis misses the mark. If it is true that the manipulation of structured rather than unstructured entities is inevitably more efficient, the question is why the language of children and adults makes use of one particular way of structuring linguistic symbols, rather than another. If any form of structuring the data would do, then the question is why children immediately converge on the 'right' way of structuring linguistic expressions, endorsing the c-command relation.

We end by cautioning the reader against interpreting our investigations of structure dependence as inherently tied to the theoretical accounts of adult language that we have considered. This is especially true for downward entailment and polarity phenomena. Even if c-command did not turn out to be the only notion that is needed to account for polarity phenomena, there are generalizations that must be stated in terms of abstract notions for which no transparent marking in the input is available.

Finally, we would like to recall the criticism to Pullum and Scholz (2002) advanced by Crain and Pietroski (2002). As we observed in Chapter 1, one of the points raised by these researchers was that children converge on generalizations that cover seemingly unrelated phenomena. In that chapter, we refined their argument and we left open the possibility that children would differ from adults in their interpretation of disjunction in sentences containing a downward entailing operator, though in limited ways. It was only after we determined that this was not the case, that we hypothesized children were indeed constructing a generalization (see Chapter 2). Once it is shown that children assign the conjunctive interpretation to sentences containing the disjunction operator *or* in the scope of negation, then children have to converge on the same notion of scope as adults. Thus, in the present chapter, we set out to determine if the relevant generalization made reference to the same primitives of adult languages. The experimental findings show that for children, just like for adults, the notion of scope is related to linguistic structure and not to an arguably simpler notion such as linear precedence. Furthermore, the findings suggest that children are capable of syntactic organization and do not entertain the shallow linguistic representations that figure prominently in the Conservative Learning model proposed by Tomasello (2000) or the Rich Input model envisioned by Pullum and Scholz (2002). Finally, the findings show that language interpretation in young children is sensitive to abstract properties, for which no overt marking in the input is available.

CHAPTER 4

Asymmetries of Child Language

The last chapter focused on the role of linguistic structure in child language. The relevance of linguistic structure for grammatical operations was used to distinguish between alternative models of language acquisition. In particular, we considered children's interpretation of disjunction in downward entailing environments as an additional phenomenon that highlights the role of structure for grammatical operations. In this chapter we put aside these broader issues, and focus on a phenomenon that has created much disagreement even among researchers that draw upon linguistic theory in their investigations of child language. In particular, we take downward entailment as a case study for theories of children's quantificational competence.

Children's interpretation of the universal quantifier is probably the most controversial topic in studies of children's semantic competence. Despite the conspicuous number of studies on the topic, there is little agreement as to how children's non-adult responses in certain tasks should be interpreted. More importantly, given the questions that are currently being asked, agreement is not within reach. Thus, it will be profitable to shift the current debate to one aspect of children's interpretation of the universal quantifier *every* that has been neglected, despite its potential significance.

4.1 The Universal Quantifier in Child Language

Children's interpretation of the universal quantifier *every* has received increasing interest in recent investigations of child language. These investigations start from the observation, due to Inhelder and Piaget (1964), that some children show a systematic non-adult response to sentences containing the universal quantifier *every*. In particular, Inhelder and Piaget (1964) discovered that some pre-school and even some school-age children reject (1) as a description of a context in which three boys are riding an elephant and there is a fourth elephant that nobody is riding.

(1)   Every boy is riding an elephant.

When children who reject (1) are asked to justify their answer, they often point to the elephant that is not being ridden by any boy. This elephant is referred to in the literature as 'the extra-object' and trials of this kind are called the 'extra-object condition.' Children who respond in this fashion in the extra-object condition appear to demand symmetry (i.e., a one-to-one relation) between the set of boys and the set of elephants. For this reason, children's non-adult rejections of (1) have come to be known as the 'symmetrical response.' The finding from the Inhelder and Piaget study has been revamped recently by a number of psycholinguists, who have proposed grammatical explanations for the phenomenon.

4.1.1 The Partial Competence View

One account of children's symmetrical response that draws upon a grammatical explanation was proposed by Philip (1995).[1] This is the Event Quantification account. The Event Quantification account attributes children's symmetrical response to a specific non-adult linguistic analysis. According to the Event Quantification account, sentences containing the universal quantifier *every* are ambiguous for children in a way they are not for adults. In addition to the adult interpretation, children can assign to these sentences an interpretation that makes (1) false in the extra-object condition. Roughly, children can analyze the universal quantifier *every* as an unselective binder, on analogy with temporal adverbs like *always* and *usually* in the adult grammar (see Lewis, 1975; Heim, 1982). In extending the analysis of adverbs to the universal quantifier, Philip (1995) contends that the determiner *every* can quantify over events in child grammar, whereas it only quantifies over individuals in the adult grammar. On the Event Quantification account, children's non-adult interpretation of the sentence *Every boy is riding an elephant* can be described as follows:

---

1 See also Roeper and De Villiers (1991).

(2)   For every event *e* in which either an elephant or a boy participates, or which is a possible sub-event of a boy-riding-an-elephant, a boy is riding an elephant in *e*.

Thus, in addition to the adult interpretation of (1), children's grammar licenses an interpretation that is more restricted than the adult interpretation. In order to make (1) true on this (non-adult) interpretation, it is not sufficient that every boy is riding an elephant. An additional requirement must be satisfied: for every elephant, there must be a boy riding that elephant. Since the 'extra-object condition' contains an elephant that is not being ridden by any boy, this requirement is not satisfied. Thus, guided by their grammar, children sometimes reject the sentence in (1) (see Philip, 1995 for a more complete explanation).

A second grammatical explanation for children's symmetrical responses was advanced by Drozd and van Loosbroek (1998; 1999). This is the Weak Quantification account. This account shares with the Event Quantification account the assumption that the source of children's non-adult responses is their grammar. The Weak Quantification account differs from the Event Quantification account in the particular non-adult grammatical analysis attributed to children (in addition to the adult interpretation). In particular, the Weak Quantification account maintains that children's non-adult interpretation of the universal quantifier *every* mirrors a possible interpretation of sentences containing the quantifier *many* in the adult language. Consider (3), from Westerståhl (1985).

(3)   Many Scandinavians have won the Nobel Prize in literature.

It has been suggested that (3) is ambiguous. One reading of (3) evaluates the number of Scandinavians who have won the Nobel Prize in literature relative to the number of Scandinavians, with *many* applying to the denotation of the subject N. The other purported reading evaluates the number of prize winners who are Scandinavian relative to the number of Nobel Prize winners, with *many* applying to the denotation of the VP. According to Drozd and van Loosbroek (1998; 1999), children's symmetrical response results from an interpretation that resembles the VP analysis that adults can give to sentences with *many*. On children's non-adult interpretation, the universal quantifier *every* applies to the set of elephants, rather than to the set of boys, as it does on the adult interpretation. In short, whereas adults interpret the sentence *Every boy is riding an elephant*, as represented in (4), children can access an additional interpretation, as in (5).

(4)   EVERY [boy] [λx (x is riding an elephant)]
        (boy ∩ λx [x riding an elephant]) ∈ EVERY (boy)

(5)   EVERY [elephant] [[λx (boy is riding x)]^2
        (elephant ∩ λx [x is ridden by a boy]) ∈ EVERY (elephant)

The semantic representation in (5) makes the sentence *Every boy is riding an elephant* true if and only if every elephant is being ridden by a boy. Under the Weak Quantification account, this analysis accounts for children's rejection of (1) in the 'extra-object' condition.

A third grammatical account of children's non-adult responses to universally quantified sentences has been proposed by Geurts (2001). This account views the origin of children's non-adult responses in a non-canonical syntax-semantics mapping. We call this the Weak Mapping account. Geurts' attempt to explain children's responses makes use of a different framework, namely Discourse Representation Theory (see Kamp, 1981; Kamp and Reyle, 1993). Technicalities aside, the main intuition exploited in Geurts' account is that strong quantifiers like *every* impose a more complex semantic representation than weak quantifiers.[3] Turning to children's non-adult responses, Geurts (2001) does not locate the problem in children's mastery of universal quantification *per se*; the problem for children lies in the fact that the mapping between form and meaning is more complex for sentences containing strong quantifiers than for ones containing weak quantifiers. Thus, the proposal by Geurts (2001) shares with the Weak Quantification account the claim that children misinterpret sentences containing the universal quantifier *every* as if it was a weak quantifier. The proposal differs from the Weak Quantification account, however, in that (a) children's 'mistakes' are expected to occur with all strong quantifiers and that (b) children are argued to fall back on the mapping that is common to (the strong usages of) all weak determiners, rather than on the

---

2 Drozd and van Loosbroek (1998; 1999) do not provide a formal representation of children's non-adult interpretation of universally quantified sentences. The interpretation in (5) is taken from Meroni et al. (2000) who attempted to represent formally Drozd and van Loosbroek's claim that children can interpret *every* on a par with the weak quantifier *many*.

3 Weak quantifiers are ones that can occur in existential *there* sentences (see Milsark, 1974, 1977). For the semantic differences between weak and strong quantifiers we refer the reader to Heim (1982).

interpretive properties that are only shown by some weak quantifiers (e.g., *few* and *many*). For present purposes we will ignore the peculiarities of the accounts proposed by Philip (1995), Drozd and van Loosbroek (1998; 1999) and Geurts (2001), and we will consider all of these accounts as variants of the Partial Competence view.

4.1.2 The Full Competence View

The need for a grammatical explanation of children's responses to sentences containing the universal quantifier *every* was questioned by Crain, Thornton, Boster, Conway, Lillo-Martin and Woodams (1996). These researchers demonstrated that children's performance dramatically improves if the experimental setting is modified. In particular, children consistently show adult-like performance if the experimental context includes some additional (kind of) animal that one of the boys considered riding (but, ultimately, even this boy rode an elephant). Crain et al. (1996) anticipated this improvement in children's performance based on the observation, from earlier research, that children's performance typically improves in the Truth Value Judgment task if certain 'felicity conditions' are satisfied in the experimental context. The claim is that some of these felicity conditions are associated with judgments of truth or falsity. More specifically, Crain et al. attribute children's consistent adult-like performance to the 'Condition of Plausible Dissent.' Crediting Russell (1948) with the relevant insight, Crain et al. (1996) maintain that the sentence in (1) is true and felicitous if, for example, some boy(s) considered riding a dinosaur but, in the end, decided against it.[4] No such alternative outcome was present in studies that evoked errors from children.

A second example of a non-linguistic account of children's non-adult responses to universally quantified sentences is offered by Freeman, Sinha and Stedmon (1982).[5] These authors focus on the circumstances in which universally quantified sentences are usually uttered. According to Freeman et al. (1982), when a speaker uses a universally quantified sentence, he requests the addressee to ensure that no relevant individual is missing. If the context does not support the *possibility* that one of these individuals might be missing, children might

---

4 Similarly, Crain et al. (1996) argue that the sentence in (1) would be false but felicitous if, for example, every boy considered riding an elephant, but some boy(s) decided to ride something else, say a dinosaur.

5 See also Freeman and Stedmon (1986).

attempt to conjure up the existence of a 'missing' individual. Going back to the extra-object condition, the extra-elephant suggests the existence of a fourth boy, corresponding to that elephant. Thus, children reject sentences like (1) in that context, because the child's mental model has been augmented to include a fourth boy, who is not riding any elephant. For present purposes we will ignore the differences between the accounts proposed by Crain et al. (1996) and Freeman et al. (1982) and we will consider both accounts as variants of the Full Competence view, since children's grammatical knowledge is exonerated from responsibility for children's 'mistakes,' which are seen to be artifacts of the pictures presented to children.

4.1.3 The Current Debate

The contrast between the Partial Competence view and the Full Competence view has received considerable attention in the literature (see Gordon, 1996; Geurts, 2000, 2001; Philip and Lynch, 2000; Sugisaki and Isobe, 2001; Gouro, Norita, Nakajima and Ariji, 2002). Most of contemporary research focuses on the particular felicity condition proposed by Crain et al. (1996) and on alternative explanations of children's improved performance in the Truth Value Judgment task. Here are two representative criticisms of the Condition of Plausible Dissent proposed by Crain et al. (1996):

> "It attempts to explain the conditioning of a strange phenomenon by means of an equally strange hypothesis. They do not define what they mean by 'felicity'.
> … This is not altogether surprising since there are no in principle falsifiable theories by means of which one can measure the 'felicity value' of an utterance. There are only intuitions about felicity…". (Philip, 1996; p. 572)

> "Contrary to what Crain et al. contend, it is doubtful that a *yes/no* question is pragmatically infelicitous unless both the affirmative and the negative answer are 'under consideration' in any substantial sense. In my own experience, children are rather good at answering all manner of questions that would be infelicitous according to Crain et al." (Geurts, 2001; p. 5)

Concerns about the specific felicity condition proposed by Crain et al. (1996) have also been proposed by researchers who do not view children's non-adult responses as resulting from non-adult linguistic principles:

"Since we have shown that adult-like responses can be obtained even in a situation where the condition of plausible dissent is not met, our results cast serious doubt on Crain et al.'s (1996) claim that the satisfaction of this condition is crucial in eliciting children's knowledge of quantification." (Sugisaki and Isobe, 2001; p. 100)

"But still, we have not obtained a comprehensive understanding of [the symmetrical response – *AG*]. There are empirical facts, for example Sugisaki and Isobe's experimental results, which the condition of plausible dissent does not suffice and we now have no clear explanation." (Gouro, Norita, Nakajima and Ariji, 2002; p. 65)

These quotes illustrate the current debate on children's understanding of the universal quantifier: the dispute revolves around the experimental manipulations that lead to children's adult performance. More generally, the debate centers on experimental methodology. No attention is paid to *research* methodology, however. Of course, features of experimental design should not be ignored. In evaluating the specific feature of design proposed by a group of researchers, though, one should not forget the research assumptions that led to that particular feature. In our view, little can be accomplished if we focus on the particular felicity conditions proposed by Freeman et al. (1982) or Crain et al. (1996) without focusing on what makes the line of research followed by these researchers attractive (see Crain et al., 1996).

In a recent review of the current debate on children's understanding of *every*, Meroni, Gualmini and Crain (2003) argued that the Full Competence view should be favored on empirical, as well as theoretical, grounds. These researchers point out that the Partial Competence view posits qualitative differences between children and adults. This conclusion is unwelcome for several reasons. First, if children differ from adults in that their grammar licenses an *additional* interpretation of sentences containing the universal quantifier *every*, it is difficult to imagine a learning mechanism that will allow children to unlearn the non-adult interpretation.[6] To date, no such mechanism has been proposed. Second, if children differ from adults in that their grammar licenses the *particular* interpretations proposed by all of the variants of the Partial Competence view we introduced, child language violates important linguistic universals uncovered by research in formal semantics, namely the compositionality of semantic interpretation and the conservativity of natural

---

6 See Meroni et al. (2000).

language determiners.[7] On this view, children's interpretation of the universal quantifier *every* would undermine the Continuity Assumption, which Meroni et al. (2003) accept as the null hypothesis for child language research (see Chapter 1). Against these difficulties for the Partial Competence view, the specific experimental maneuver proposed by Crain et al. (1996) bears very little importance. Consistent with the argument of Meroni et al., we would like to scrutinize the Partial Competence view by focusing on the assumptions endorsed by the Partial Competence view. Here we focus on one such assumption.

4.2 A Common Assumption behind the Partial Competence View

The variants of the Partial Competence view introduced in Section 4.1.1 present important differences. In the remainder of this chapter, we put aside the peculiarities of these accounts, and we focus on an assumption that is common to all of them. For expository purposes, it will be useful to recall the construction under consideration.

(6)   Every boy is riding an elephant.

A simplified logical form for (6) is represented as follows:

(7)   EVERY [boy] [λx (x is riding an elephant)]

By looking at (7), one can view the universal quantifier *every* as a function that takes two arguments, namely the semantic value of the noun phrase *boy* and the semantic value of the verbal phrase *is riding an elephant*. In set theoretic terms, the function expressed by the universal quantifier makes the sentence true if the set of boys is a subset of the set of elephant riders. On this view, the logical form of (6) contributes to the semantic interpretation in a transparent fashion.[8] The noun phrase that combines with the universal quantifier *every* in (6) is taken to be its first argument in the semantic representation in (7), i.e., its restrictor; in

---

7 We will discuss the relevance of conservativity for determiner meanings in the concluding section of the present chapter.

8 The logical form can be derived from the underlying syntactic structure after the application of quantifier raising (see May, 1977) or noun prefixing (see Heim, 1982).

the same transparent fashion, the verb phrase is taken to be its second argument, i.e., its nuclear scope.[9]

The Event Quantification account, the Weak Quantification account and the Weak Mapping account, however, assume that children can access an additional interpretation of (6) in which the two arguments of the universal quantifier *every* are not constrained by the syntactic structure of the sentence in the same transparent way. As we have seen, the Event Quantification account maintains that children can also access the interpretation in (2), reported below as (8).

(8)   For every event *e* in which either an elephant or a boy participates, or which is a possible sub-event of a boy-riding-an-elephant, a boy is riding an elephant in *e*.

The semantic representation in (8) does not restrict the application of the universal quantifier *every* to the events to which a boy participates. Rather, the semantic representation in (8) extends the application of the universal quantifier *every* to events to which an elephant participates. In other words, the restrictor of the universal quantifier contains the semantic value of the noun that combines with the universal quantifier *every* in the overt syntax (i.e., *boy*) and also the semantic value of the noun phrase in object position in the overt syntax (i.e., *elephant*).

In analogous fashion, the Weak Quantification account maintains that children's interpretation of sentences containing the universal quantifier *every* disregards the syntactic structure of the sentence under consideration (see (9)).

(9)   EVERY [elephant] [[λx (boy is riding x)]

In addition to the adult interpretation, children can in fact resort to an interpretation in which the direct object is taken as the first argument (i.e., the restrictor) of the universal quantifier *every*.

Finally, recall the Weak Mapping account proposed by Geurts (2001). On this account, children's non-adult interpretation emerges when their attention is drawn to the set of elephants. The resulting interpretation is as follows:

(10)   [y: elephant(y)]<every>[x: boy(x) is riding y]

---

9 We refer the reader to Diesing (1992) for an explicit model of the syntax-semantics mapping.

Thus, on the non-adult interpretation, children construct the representation that corresponds to a strong use of weak determiners and they may, therefore, choose the set denoted by either noun phrase as presupposed.

In sum, most variants of the Partial Competence view share the assumption that children can resort to an interpretation that disregards the adult mapping between overt syntax and semantic interpretation. Here are a few passages from studies that endorse the grammatical view of children's non-adult interpretation of the universal quantifier:

> "The WQH [Weak Quantification Hypothesis] claims that children assign a weak-quantifier interpretation to universal quantifiers. This predicts that a child's interpretations of universal quantifiers can be affected by the meaning of other constituents in the sentence, or what the children know about the denotations of those constituents." (Drozd, 2000; p. 358)

> "My proposal is based on an old idea, viz. that children's errors are caused by a non-canonical mapping from syntactic form to semantic representation." (Geurts, 2001; p. 1)

> "All that matters for semantic interpretation of the universal quantifier in such a representation is that this quantifier have scope over the entire sentence: its original position in surface structure is completely irrelevant." (Philip, 1995; p. 50)[10]

Similar views seem to be endorsed by researchers who do not propose a linguistic account of children's 'mistakes:'

> "This paper will argue that there is a type of sentence interpretation, occurring under certain circumstances and in certain age groups, in which a subject-predicate distinction between the content words is not properly registered. The sentence is encoded as a simple string or unordered set of substantive words without hierarchical structure." (Bucci, 1978; p. 58)

---

10 This quote is taken from Philip's discussion of possible explanations for children's preference for the event interpretation of universally quantified sentences and may not represent Philip's position. However, we believe that the analysis attributed to children by Philip (1995) can be described by the quoted paragraph.

"In the absence of a decisive structuring of language, it is then the structuring of the physical array [visual input] that determines the outcome." (Donaldson and Lloyd, 1974; p. 82, taken from Philip, 1995; p. 40)

These quotes highlight the underlying assumption, namely that the interface between syntax and semantics assumes different guises in child and adult language. We call this the Mis-mapping hypothesis

The empirical predictions of the Mis-mapping hypothesis are worth pursuing. If children differ from adults in the way the syntactic representation of an expression dictates its semantic interpretation, there is little hope for a characterization of child language that draws upon the principles of linguistic theory. If children differ from adults in the particular way the modular architecture of the language faculty is implemented, one wonders whether children's adult-like behavior *ever* results from adult-like representations. On this view, it might be argued that differences between children and adults are not necessarily limited to cases in which children and adults give different responses to a given task. A worrisome example of this position is offered by Bucci (1978), who argued that children sometimes give the correct response for the wrong reasons in experiments assessing their interpretation of universally quantified sentences:

"The data suggest that where young children appear to respond logically to universal affirmative propositions in natural language situations, they might be relying on pragmatic *rather than grammatical representations*." (Bucci, 1978; p. 74 - emphasis mine)

It is important to consider the implications of the Mis-mapping hypothesis for other phenomena. For example, we have discussed children's adult-like responses to sentences containing the negative quantifier *None of the Ns* in Chapter 2. Now, should we qualify our conclusions? Should we consider the possibility that children might have shown adult-like behavior because their failure to map syntax to semantics does not yield any truth-conditional difference with intersective quantifiers like *None of the Ns*? If the Mis-mapping hypothesis is correct, there is a real possibility that children's adult-like responses *never* reflect adult-like operations.

The Mis-mapping hypothesis is worth scrutinizing for yet another reason: it cannot be incorporated into an independently justified model of language processing, the Modularity Matching model (see Crain and Thornton, 1998; Crain and Wexler, 1999). According to the Modularity Matching model, operations within the language faculty are hierarchically organized, such that operations of higher level components apply to the output of lower level components (also see Crain and Steedman, 1985). When it comes to the interfaces between different modules of the language faculty, the Modularity Matching model prescribes taking an extremely constrained stand on the possible relations among components of the language apparatus. If multiple outputs are transferred from one level to another, then principles at higher levels will maintain or reject outputs from lower levels. However, principles at higher levels can only evaluate the particular outputs licensed by lower levels, and cannot generate novel representations. For example, Crain and Steedman (1985) spelled out these modular assumptions about the syntax/semantics interface using the adage "syntax proposes, semantics disposes." According to the Mis-mapping hypothesis, however, when the output of the syntax module is shunted to the semantics module, a new interpretation can be generated.

Sentences containing the universal quantifier provide a fertile testing ground for the Mis-mapping hypothesis. For intersective quantifiers like *no* or *some*, the failure to correctly represent the two arguments may not yield any truth-conditional differences. Consider the quantifier *no*. Roughly, a sentence of the form *No As are Bs* is true if and only if the intersection between the set of *As* and the set of *Bs* is empty. Since set-intersection is a symmetric relation, the order with which these sets are considered is irrelevant. The same holds for the determiner *some*, which demands a non-empty intersection.

Now consider *every*. Roughly, a sentence of the form *Every A is a B* is true if and only if the set of *As* is a subset of the set of entities that have the property expressed by *B*. Thus, in determining whether *Every A is a B* is true, the first step is to zoom in on the relevant sets. Then, one has to ensure that set-inclusion holds. Importantly, set inclusion is not a symmetric relationship. Thus, the order with which these sets are considered is relevant for the interpretation of sentences of this form. As a consequence, in order to evaluate sentences containing the universal quantifier *every*, one must consider the relevant sets in the particular 'order' specified by the syntax. This, according to the Mis-mapping hypothesis is beyond children's capacities, however. According to the Mis-mapping hypothesis, children either ignore or fail to construct a semantic representation as dictated by the syntax. Thus, a prediction of the Mis-mapping hypothesis is that children should fail to display adult-like knowledge of all the phenomena that make reference to that representation. In other words, a prediction of the Mis-mapping hypothesis is that children should fail to display adult-like knowledge of all the phenomena that distinguish between the two arguments of the universal quantifier *every*. To investigate this prediction, we turn to children's knowledge of the differences between the two arguments of the universal quantifier *every*: the direction of entailment relations.

4.3 The Universal Asymmetry of the Universal Quantifier

The properties of downward entailing operators were discussed in Chapter 2. Here, we focus on the relevance of downward entailment as it pertains to the interpretation of the universal quantifier. The universal quantifier *every* presents an interesting peculiarity: it is downward entailing on its first argument, but upward entailing on its second argument. This asymmetry is suggested by all the properties of downward entailment that we reviewed in Chapter 2. First, only the first argument of *every* licenses inferences from a set to its subsets (as long as the relevant presuppositions are satisfied).

(11)   a.   Every boy who ate <u>pizza</u> got sick
                 $\Rightarrow$ Every boy who ate <u>pepperoni pizza</u> got sick.
         b.   Every boy ate <u>pizza</u>
                 *$\Rightarrow$ Every boy ate <u>pepperoni pizza</u>.

Second, only the first argument licenses the occurrence of NPIs like *any* or *ever*.

(12)   a.   Every boy who ate <u>any</u> pizza got sick.
         b.   *Every boy ate <u>any</u> pizza.

(13)   a.   Every boy who <u>ever</u> ate pizza got sick.
         b.   *Every boy <u>ever</u> ate pizza.

Finally, only the first argument of the universal quantifier *every* licenses the conjunctive interpretation of the disjunction operator *or*.

(14)   a.   Every boy who ate cheese pizza <u>or</u> pepperoni pizza got sick
                 $\Leftrightarrow$ Every boy who ate cheese pizza got sick <u>and</u> every boy who ate pepperoni pizza got sick.
         b.   Every boy ate cheese pizza <u>or</u> pepperoni pizza
                 *$\Leftrightarrow$ Every boy ate cheese pizza <u>and</u> every boy ate pepperoni pizza.

The examples above provide us with a useful pattern, for several purposes. First of all, the behavior of the first argument of *every* constitutes an exception to the hypothesis that downward entailment is limited to negative-like contexts. The question is whether children make that hypothesis. In addition, one would like to investigate whether children know that the two arguments of the universal quantifier *every* differ in the direction of entailment relations. This research question assumes particular importance for evaluating the various grammatical accounts of children's non-adult responses to sentences containing the universal quantifier *every*. As we have seen in Section 4.2, a common assumption of these accounts is that children experience difficulty in the syntax/semantics mapping of sentences containing the universal quantifier *every*. As a result of this difficulty, children are expected to fail to represent the two arguments of the universal quantifier at the semantic level (as dictated by the syntax). A consequence of this is that children should fail to show adult-like knowledge of any phenomenon that hinges upon the correct semantic representation of the universal quantifier *every*. Thus, a prediction of the Mis-mapping hypothesis is that children should not master any of the properties exemplified in (11) through (14), since all of those properties require that the two arguments of the universal quantifier *every* are kept distinct.

In order to evaluate this prediction, two features of children's knowledge need to be determined. First, it needs to be determined whether children know that the first argument of the universal quantifier *every* constitutes a downward entailing environment. Second, it needs to be determined whether children know that the second argument of the universal quantifier *every* does *not* constitute a downward entailing environment. Let us consider how these issues have been investigated in previous studies.

A relevant study was conducted by Gualmini, Meroni and Crain (2003). These researchers carried out a Truth Value Judgment task to determine whether children correctly interpret the disjunction operator in accordance with the inference scheme typical of downward entailment, when *or* occurs in the first argument of *every*. In one of the trials, children were told a story about five trolls who went to the fast food restaurant owned by Genie. One troll ordered a big hot-dog, two trolls ordered onion rings and two trolls ordered French fries. At the end of the story, Genie gave some mustard to the two trolls who ordered French fries, but he gave ketchup to the trolls who had ordered onion rings. At this point children were presented with the sentence in (15).

(15)   Every troll who ordered French fries or onion rings got some mustard.

Notice that (15) receives a different truth value in the context described in the story, depending on whether children assign the conjunctive interpretation to the disjunction operator *or*. In particular, if children correctly apply the inference scheme typical of downward entailing environments (see (16)), they should reject the target sentence on the grounds that the trolls who ordered onion rings did not receive any mustard.

(16)   Every troll who ordered French fries or onion rings got some mustard.

⇔   Every troll who ordered French fries got some mustard and every troll who ordered onion rings got some mustard.

By contrast, if children fail to apply the inference scheme typical of downward entailing environments, they could follow the inference scheme in (17), which would compel them to accept the target sentence; even though the trolls who ordered onion rings did not receive any mustard, the ones who ordered French fries did.

(17)   Every troll who ordered French fries or onion rings got some mustard.

*⇔   Every troll who ordered French fries got some mustard or every troll who ordered onion rings got some mustard.

Turning to the results, twenty children ranging in age from 3;11 to 5;08 were interviewed. These children rejected the target sentences 95% of the time. When asked to indicate "what really happened," children pointed out that the puppet was wrong because the trolls who had ordered onion rings had not received any mustard. Thus, children's responses, as well as their justifications, suggest that they were interpreting the target sentence in accordance with the inference scheme typical of downward entailing environments (i.e., (16)). Let us now turn to the second argument of *every*.

The logical properties of the second argument of the universal quantifier *every* were investigated by Boster and Crain (1993). As reviewed in Chapter 2, these researchers investigated children's interpretation of sentences containing disjunction in the nuclear scope of the universal quantifier *every*. The research question addressed in the Boster and Crain study was whether children would extend the application of the (relevant) De Morgan's law to *non*-downward entailing environments. In order to address this question, Boster and Crain (1993) designed a Truth Value Judgment task employing the Prediction Mode (see Chierchia et al., 1998). Children were asked to evaluate sentences like (18) in various scenarios.

(18)   Every ghostbuster will choose a cat or a pig.

The results obtained by Boster and Crain (1993) provide evidence that children do not treat the nuclear scope of the universal quantifier *every* as downward entailing. In other words, children do not interpret (18) as equivalent to (19).

(19)   Every ghostbuster will choose a cat and every ghostbuster will choose a pig.

The experimental findings show that children do not extend the pattern of inference that characterizes downward entailing environments to *non*-DE environments. However, it is pertinent to observe that Boster and Crain (1993) discovered some non-adult behavior in children's interpretation of the sentences under investigation. In particular, children generally accepted (18) in a context in which every ghostbuster had chosen exactly one object. However, almost every child imposed an additional restriction on the interpretation of (18). One group of children expected (the kind of) animal chosen by the ghostbusters to be the same for all ghostbusters, and a second group of children expected the (kind of) animal chosen by the ghostbusters *not* to be the same for all ghostbusters. We will return to these 'mistakes' shortly. For the present purposes, we would like to emphasize that, despite some non-adult behavior, children never applied the inference scheme typical of downward entailing environments when interpreting *or* in the second argument of the universal quantifier.

Taken together, the results of Gualmini et al. (2003) and the findings by Boster and Crain (1993) reveal an asymmetry between children's interpretation of the disjunction operator *or* in the two arguments of the universal quantifier *every*. This asymmetry, in our view, reflects children's knowledge of the difference between the two arguments of the universal quantifier. By inference, the findings are unanticipated by the Mis-mapping hypothesis. Children have correct understanding of the meaning of the universal quantifier *every* and all of its consequences.

In deference to a debate that centers on experimental methodology, we wish to raise some potential problems in comparing the results obtained by Boster and Crain (1993) and those obtained by Gualmini, Meroni and Crain (2003). First and foremost, the two studies employed different variants of the Truth Value Judgment task. Boster and Crain (1993) adopted the Prediction Mode, whereas

Gualmini et al. (2003) adopted the Description Mode. Within a debate on research methodology, this difference is not optimal for purposes of data comparison. Second, the results reported by Boster and Crain (1993) yielded a rather complicated picture. As we said, children did not seem to access the conjunctive interpretation of the disjunction operator *or*. However, most children unexpectedly rejected the target sentences. Boster and Crain (1993) argued that this pattern is the result of an additional restriction on the adult interpretation by children. The vast majority of children, however, showed a pattern of responses different from that of adults. Furthermore, children's behavior in the Boster and Crain study differed from adults' in *two* ways, thereby making any comparison across experiments all the more problematic. Third, children's adult-like responses in experiments involving universally quantified sentences have been recently attributed to the difference in salience of the relevant objects.[11] Ideally, one would like to address this issue as well. For all these reasons, we return to the laboratory.

4.4 Experimental Design

4.4.1 Experiment IV

To minimize the difficulties that arise when comparing the results of Boster and Crain (1993) and Gualmini et al. (2003), we conducted a Truth Value Judgment task. The experiment investigated the same construction investigated by Boster and Crain (1993), namely sentences containing the disjunction *or* in the second argument of the universal quantifier *every*. The experiment differed from the one reported in Boster and Crain (1993), however, in two respects. First, the present experiment adopted the Description Mode of the Truth Value Judgment task, thus making it easier to compare the findings with those from the Gualmini et al. study. Second, the experimental contexts were constructed to take into consideration the non-adult pattern uncovered by Boster and Crain (1993). The reader might recall that most children required that at least one ghostbuster chose a pig and that at least one ghostbuster chose a cat when interpreting sentences like (20).

---

11 See Gordon (1996) for this hypothesis and Meroni et al. (2000) for some empirical evidence against such a hypothesis.

(20)   Every ghostbuster will choose a cat or a pig.

Children who showed this kind of interpretation were called *Diversity Children* by Boster and Crain (1993).[12] Since this pattern accounted for the majority of children's 'mistakes,' the experimental context of our own experiment was designed so that the requirement imposed by the diversity children would be met. In addition, the context was designed so that children would reject the target sentence if they assigned the conjunctive interpretation to the disjunction *or*.[13] In a typical trial, children were told the following story.

(21)   "This is a story about Chucky who is the director of the circus and three kids. There are a lot of animals in the circus: a snake, a pig, two small dinosaurs and one big dinosaur, two regular tigers and one big white tiger. Chucky is very worried because the animal trainer has left and the show is about to begin, so he asks his friends if they could help him: "You guys come here all the time, you must have learned some tricks. Do you think you can help me?" The first kid says: "Sure, I'll help you, I always play with the dinosaurs" and he takes one of the two small dinosaurs. The second kid says: "I will help you, Chucky! I spent a lot of time with the tigers and the dinosaurs, so I'll take one of each." And he takes the second small dinosaur and one of the regular tigers. The third kid looks at the animals that are left and says: "Well, maybe I should choose a different animal, but this snake looks so scary and I do not think I can get that pig to do any tricks!" Then he considers choosing the white tiger and the big dinosaur but says "No, I can't do any tricks with these animals. They are too big for me!" and takes the second regular tiger."

At this point, the puppet offered his description of the story, as follows:

---

12 Boster and Crain (1993) tested fifteen children ranging in age from 3;6 to 4;8, with a mean age of 4;8. Of these fifteen children, Boster and Crain (1993) classified 10 children as *diversity children*.

13 The context does not meet the restriction imposed by the children who Boster and Crain called *conformity children*. Thus, it is possible that some children would reject the target sentence because they required all the relevant characters to choose the same animal. We will consider this possibility after we present the experimental results.

(22)   This was a story about Chucky and his friends and I know what
        happened. <u>Every kid took a tiger or a dinosaur.</u>

Let us consider the description offered by the puppet. If children do not know
that the second argument of the universal quantifier *every* is upward entailing,
they should access the conjunctive interpretation of the disjunction operator *or*
as in (23):

(23)   Every kid took a tiger <u>and</u> every kid took a dinosaur.

The interpretation in (23) makes the target sentence false in the context under
consideration, however. In particular, the target sentence is false because the
first kid only took a dinosaur and because the third kid only chose a tiger. The
context was designed so that children should also reject the target sentence if
they failed to restrict the application of *every* to the set of boys. In particular, if
children demand a one-to-one correspondence between the set of dinosaurs and
tigers and the set of boys, they should reject the target sentence on the grounds
that one tiger and one dinosaur were not chosen by any boy (i.e., the white tiger
and the big dinosaur considered by the third kid at the end of the story). By
contrast, if children know that the second argument of the universal quantifier
every is upward entailing, they should accept the target sentence on the grounds
that every kid did choose one of the animals mentioned in the target sentence.

    Twenty-three children participated in the experiment. They ranged in age
from 3;10 to 5;09 (mean age: 5;0). Each child was presented with four target
trials ant four fillers to balance the number of 'yes' and 'no' responses. Turning
to the results, children accepted the target sentence 65 times out of 92 trials
(71%). A control group of 8 adults participated in a videotaped version of the
experiment. They accepted the target sentences 84% of the time (27/32) (see the
Appendix for more experimental details). It is pertinent to observe that, among
the 27 cases of non-adult rejection, in 11 such cases children pointed out that
Kermit was wrong because of only one of the relevant characters. Importantly,
when these children were asked to arrange the toys 'to make Kermit right' they
only moved one object (e.g., they would give a tiger to the first kid in the story
in (21), or a dinosaur to the third kid, but not both). [14] Thus, taking into

---

14 This kind of response probably corresponds to the behavior of the children
described as *conformity kids* by Boster and Crain (1993). Taking the story in (21), these
children required that the boys of the story did not differ with respect to one of the

consideration children's justification of their negative responses, the percentage of responses that are consistent with the adult interpretation of the disjunction operator *or* raises to 83%. In addition, three of children's non-adult responses were motivated by pointing to the kid that had two animals. This response is apparently dictated by the computation of an implicature triggered by the disjunction *or*.[15] Thus, we are left with only 13 cases of unexplained non-adult responses (14%). Among these cases, children pointed only 3 times to both relevant characters in the story (i.e., the kid who only had a tiger and the kid who only had a dinosaur).[16]

Thus, the pattern of results in the present study confirms the existence of some difficulties in children's interpretation of sentences containing the disjunction operator in the second argument of the universal quantifier *every*. Importantly, most of these difficulties mirror the pattern of behavior uncovered by Boster and Crain (1993). Children's non-occurring responses are equally informative. First, as we saw, children almost never assigned the conjunctive interpretation to (sentences containing) the disjunction *or* in the second argument of the universal quantifier. Second, children never produced a symmetrical response. In other words, children never pointed out that the target sentence was false because one of the tigers (i.e., the white tiger) or one of the dinosaurs (i.e., the big dinosaur) had not been chosen.

The findings allow us to carry out a more productive comparison between children's interpretation of disjunction in the two arguments of the universal quantifier *every*. This comparison yields an asymmetry. Children, like adults, know that the first argument of the universal quantifier *every* is downward entailing, and they know that the second argument is not. Knowledge of this asymmetry follows from the knowledge of the meaning of the universal quantifier *every* (and the meaning of *or*). More pertinent for present purposes, knowledge of the asymmetry in the entailment patterns entails children's ability to maintain the two arguments of the universal quantifier *every* distinct.

---

animals mentioned in the target sentence. It is important to recall that conformity children amounted to one fourth of the experiment participants in the Boster and Crain study.

15 In short, the children inferred from the use of *or* that the stronger statement *Every kid took a tiger and a dinosaur* did not hold and assumed that no kid should have both a tiger and a dinosaur.

16 Recall that in the first argument of *every* the conjunctive interpretation of disjunction accounted for 95% of children's responses (see Gualmini et al., 2003).

4.5 Conclusion

Over the past few years, research has focused on various aspects of children's semantic competence, including quantification. In this chapter we have attempted to assess children's semantic competence by drawing upon the semantic property of downward entailment. In particular, we have argued that children's mastery of downward entailment extends to one of its most surprising features, namely the asymmetry between the two arguments of the universal quantifier *every*. We saw evidence that children distinguish between the two arguments of the universal quantifier *every*. This finding is not surprising if one adopts the Full Competence view defended by Crain et al. (1996), but it is unanticipated on the view that children experience difficulties in the mapping between the syntactic and the semantic representation of sentences containing the universal quantifier *every*.

The findings allow us to draw two related conclusions. First, children know the semantics of the universal quantifier *every*. In other words, they know that the meaning expressed by *every* can be represented as the set-theoretic operation of set-inclusion. Second, children know how to order the relevant sets. In other words, they know that the sets between which set-theoretic inclusion must hold have to be chosen taking the syntactic structure of the sentence under consideration.

The relevance of the findings extends beyond the current debate on children's interpretation of the universal quantifier *every*. In particular, we drew attention earlier to the fact that the first argument of *every* does not share the negative flavor that most downward entailing environments exhibit. Furthermore, the universal quantifier *every* stands out against the majority of quantifiers in that its two arguments exhibit opposite behavior. The findings suggest that, once again, children's knowledge exceeds the data. It is hard to see what learning mechanism would allow children to learn the (difference in) entailment relations of the two arguments of a quantificational expression. In the case of *every*, the difficulty is confounded by the fact that *every* is the only quantifier whose arguments behave in opposite ways. In absence of guidance from Universal Grammar, it is difficult to see how children could successfully master this asymmetry.

The role of Universal Grammar for children's knowledge of quantification has been recently questioned by Geurts (2000). This is how Geurts puts it:

"But what *are* the precepts of Universal Grammar with respect to universal quantification? There are many ways of answering this question. It might be held (i) that the logical concept of universal quantification is innate; or that (ii) that the syntactic structures for expressing universal quantification are innate; or (iii) that the syntax-semantics mapping required for the interpretation of universally quantified sentences is innate; or (iv) that several of (i) through (iii) are true; and so forth. But none of these claims seems very promising to me, because I don't see why Universal Grammar should have anything specific to say on the subject of universal quantification (or quantification *tout court*, for that matter)." (Geurts, 2000; p. 528, italics in text)

In our view, all of (i)-(iii) must be true. Any weaker position would be left hard pressed to propose a learning mechanism that would allow children to converge on the adult grammar.

In fact, Universal Grammar must have a lot to say about quantification. We have briefly touched upon one relevant property of UG, which is a putative semantic universal, namely the conservativity of determiner meanings. If Universal Grammar did not have anything to say about quantification tout court, it would be difficult to explain conservativity. If children's hypothesis space is constrained by Universal Grammar, by contrast, the conservativity of determiner meanings in adult languages follows from the fact that UG prohibits any child from entertaining a non-conservative meaning for any determiner. For, if children did not obey this constraint, then we should find some non-conservative determiner meaning in some adult-language, contrary to fact.

The role of Universal Grammar in constraining determiner meanings allows us to discuss a few related issues. First, it is instructive to relate conservativity to other facts about natural languages, in the same way we have discussed the correlation between the different consequences of downward entailment (e.g., the licensing of inferences from sets to subsets and the conjunctive interpretation of the disjunction operator *or*). Second, the conservativity of determiner meanings provides us with a clear illustration of a domain-specific problem. Let us consider each fact in turn, starting from conservativity.

As observed by Meroni et al. (2000), the non-adult interpretation attributed to children by proponents of the Partial Competence view violates conservativity (see Barwise and Cooper, 1981; Keenan and Stavi, 1986). The relevant definition is reported below:

(24)   A determiner meaning is conservative iff:
$B \in DET(A)$ iff $(B \cap A) \in DET(A)$
(where A, B are sets, DET is a function from sets into sets of sets,
and $\cap$ = set intersection)

A way to illustrate the conservativity of determiner meanings amounts to showing that determiners generate inferences according to the following scheme, where A represents (the denotation of) the NP that combines with the determiner and B represents (the denotation of) the VP.

(25) $D(A)(B) \Leftrightarrow D(A)(A \cap B)$

The following examples illustrate that *few*, *every*, *no*, and *most* express conservative meanings.

(26)   a.   Few Italians eat sushi
                $\Leftrightarrow$ Few Italians are Italians who eat sushi.
    b.   Every Italian eats pasta
                $\Leftrightarrow$ Every Italian is an Italian who eats pasta.
    c.   No Italians eat peanut butter
                $\Leftrightarrow$ No Italians are Italians who eat peanut butter.
    d.   Most Italians drink wine
                $\Leftrightarrow$ Most Italians are Italians who drink wine.

So far, the conservativity of determiner meanings amounts to a descriptive generalization. To date, no explanation has been advanced for this recurrent regularity. A notable exception is given by Fox (2002) who credits Yoad Winter and Gennaro Chierchia with the relevant insight. Fox (2002) argues that a promising research strategy links the conservativity of determiner meanings to the copy theory of movement (see Chomsky, 1995). On this view, the equivalence in (25) follows from the fact that at some level of abstraction the noun phrase that combines with the determiner is indeed interpreted in two places.[17] Unfortunately, this line of research has not yet been fully developed.

---

17 Although potentially different from the scenario envisioned by Fox (2002), a clearer illustration comes from quantifiers in subject position. On the VP-internal subject hypothesis, one could argue that the subject noun phrase is indeed interpreted in two

Nevertheless, it is clear that linguistic theory should provide an explanation for the conservativity of determiner meanings.

In light of these observations, it might be true that Universal Grammar does not have anything to say about quantification. Not because quantification can manifest itself in an unbounded number of ways across natural languages, but rather, because what Universal Grammar has to say about quantification follows from what Universal Grammar has to say in other domains.

Similar considerations apply to the possible patterns of entailment. As we introduced the pattern of entailments generated by *every*, we observed an asymmetry. The first argument of *every* is downward entailing, while its second argument is not.[18] Thus, the entailment pattern of *every* sets this determiner aside from all other monotone quantifiers, which are either downward entailing on both arguments (e.g., *no*) or on neither argument (e.g., *some*). Against the background provided by intersective quantifiers like *no* and *some*, the class of determiners like *every* certainly emerges as an anomaly. Once we acknowledge the existence of determiners like *every*, however, the lack of any determiner showing the opposite pattern provides us with a second anomaly. The question is why there is no determiner which is downward entailing on its second argument, and upward entailing on its first argument. This is exactly the kind of question that brings linguistic theory and language acquisition together. From the perspective of the acquisitionist, the question is how the child avoids the mistake of assuming that some determiner could be downward entailing on its second argument, but upward entailing on its first argument. Consider the table below:

---

positions: one external to the verbal phrase (i.e., the restrictor of the quantifier) and one internal to the verbal phrase (i.e., internal to the nuclear scope).

18 Of course, similar considerations apply to other determiners that share the 'core' meaning of universal quantification, e.g., *each* and *all*.

(27)

	1st Argument Downward Entailing	1st Argument Upward Entailing
2nd Argument Downward Entailing	*No, neither*	-
2nd Argument Upward Entailing	*Every, both*	*Some,* numerals

As the table in (27) illustrates, the logical space of monotonic quantifiers consists of four options (see van Benthem, 1984). Yet, one of these options never appears to be realized by a simple determiner (see Horn, 1989; and Hoecksema, 1999).[19] All options are realized except for one. How does the child avoid that option? How can the child project beyond the primary linguistic data without incurring in the mistake of assuming that some determiner would fill the empty cell of the table above. Notice that it is perfectly possible to find a complex expression that would fill that empty cell. For example, if we attribute the meaning conveyed by negation and *every* to a single lexical expression (indicated as NOTEVERY), we see that the desired inferences go through (see Horn, 1989 for discussion).

(28)   NOTEVERY European likes wine.
        'Not every European likes wine'

(29)   NOTEVERY European likes wine
              *⇒   NOTEVERY Italian likes wine.
        'Not every European likes wine'
              *⇒   'not every Italian likes wine'

---

19 A lexical expression that appears to violate conservativity and to instantiate the pattern of entailment under consideration is *only*. However, I assume that *only* is not a determiner (see Chierchia and McConnel-Ginet, 1990).

(30)   NOTEVERY European likes wine.
              ⇒   NOTEVERY European likes red wine
        'Not every European likes wine'
              ⇒   'Not every European likes red wine'

Thus, it is possible to come up with an expression that shows the opposite pattern of *every*. But natural language determiners do not exploit this possibility.[20] Nor do children ever conceive of this, as far as we know. If Universal Grammar did not have anything to say about quantification, including the possible entailment patterns of determiners, this would be totally unexplained.

Let us now turn to the relevance of the findings discussed in the present chapter for input-based models of language acquisition such as the Conservative Learning model and the Rich Input model introduced in Chapter 1. We have shown that children's semantic competence of the universal quantifier *every* runs deep. Not only can children correctly interpret universally quantified sentences like *Every boy is riding an elephant* when the relevant felicity conditions are satisfied. Children can also interpret arguably more complicated sentences like *Every troll who ordered French fries or onion rings got some mustard* and *Every kid picked a dinosaur or a tiger*.

The findings confirm that young children know that the interpretation of *or* can be affected by some abstract property of the environment in which it occurs, namely downward entailment. Again, no structure independent notion can explain the conditions under which children assign the conjunctive interpretation to disjunction in universally quantified sentences.

It might be tempting to interpret our arguments as if we excluded *any* differences between children's and adults' interpretation of universally quantified sentences. Our point is simply that there are no differences between children's and adults' interpretation of universally quantified sentences that would violate core principles of Universal Grammar. It is possible, of course,

---

20 It is important to observe that the same point can be made regardless of whether one follows a syntactic or a semantic characterization of entailment patterns (see discussion in Ludlow, 2002). Even on a syntactic account like the one proposed by Ludlow (2002), where the interpretation of determiners directly follows from the features introduced by that determiner, the question is why only certain clusters of features can be introduced.

that children might differ from adults in what the relevant entities are, *but only in limited ways*. Consider (31) again.

(31)   Every boy is riding an elephant.

It is possible that children and adults might differ in what they conceive the contextually relevant boys to be. Thus, children might restrict the domain of quantification of *every* to one subset of the boys in the context, whereas adults might restrict the domain to a different (sub)set of boys, in the same context. However, the semantics of natural language determiners is such that, in felicitous contexts, differences could pertain only to the relevant *subset* of the boys available in the context.[21]

Finally, let us consider the domain-specificity of the task. Assuming that language acquisition is constrained by Universal Grammar does not say anything about how children manage to map the correct meanings onto the sounds they are exposed to. In the particular case at hand, assuming that children can only entertain conservative determiner meanings does not explain how each English determiner comes to have the particular conservative meaning that it comes to have. The child has to learn the meaning of each particular determiner form.

In the word learning literature, it is often argued that word learning proceeds through some form of domain general learning mechanism (see Smith, 1999).[22] We believe that determiners provide a clear challenge for this view. The case of determiners is particularly interesting because it shows that children's task is not really to learn the meaning of any given words. Rather, the task is to learn the meaning of any given word as constrained by Universal Grammar. In the case at hand, the task is to learn the meaning of any given word as constrained by the syntactic class to which that word belongs. One can easily find meanings, that children eventually learn, that look suspiciously similar to non-conservative determiner meanings. One recurring example is that of the adverb *only*. A second example is given by the adjective *equinumerous*, which also expresses a relationship between (the members of) two sets. Yet, *equinumerous* expresses a relationship between two sets that would violate conservativity if *equinoumerous* were a determiner. Thus, the child's task is not to learn whether a certain word has the meaning expressed by *equinumerous*. The task of the child is to learn whether a certain word has the meaning

---

21 See von Fintel (1994) for quantifiers restrictions in adult languages.
22 See Bloom (2000) and Waxman (2002) for recent overviews of word learning.

expressed by *equinumerous*, once the child has established that that word is not a determiner. If the child has established that a particular word is a determiner, the problem does not arise. If the child has established that the word under consideration is a determiner, the set-theoretic relationship expressed by *equinumerous* is not even an option. Similar considerations probably apply to any set theoretic relations that would cause a determiner to be downward entailing on its second argument, but not on its first argument. Again, this seems to be a quirk of natural language determiners. Thus, even if word learning might proceed through domain-general mechanisms, Universal Grammar must hold those mechanisms in check. All of a sudden, it does not look like domain-general learning anymore.

CHAPTER 5

Structure and Beyond

The last two chapters described various studies showing children's adult-like knowledge of polarity phenomena. Our discussion began with some findings from previous research, reviewed in Chapter 2. The discussion has so far ignored other findings, however. In particular, we have not followed up on Musolino's discovery concerning children's non-adult interpretation of the positive polarity item *some*. As the reader may recall, Musolino (1998) found that English-speaking children, unlike adults, tend to interpret object noun phrases containing *some* within the scope of negation. This discovery is surprising, in light of our investigations of children's knowledge of downward entailment. Focusing on the interpretation of indefinites, the experimental evidence leads to an impasse. Children's comprehension and production of the negative polarity item *any* appears to conform to the target grammar from the earliest stages of language development. However, the same does not hold for children's production and understanding of *some*, the positive counterpart of *any*. This chapter returns to this piece of the puzzle.

5.1 Children's Interpretation of Quantifiers in Negative Sentences

In recent years, research on children's interpretation of quantifiers has extended to negative sentences. Consider the example below.

(1)   The detective didn't find some guys.[1]

It is generally assumed that (1) requires a wide scope interpretation for the existentially quantified object *some guys*. In other words, the most natural – if

---

1 Recall that we are only interested in the stressed variant of *some*.

not the only - interpretation of (1) can be paraphrased as meaning that there are some guys such that the detective didn't find them (i.e., *some* > *not*).

As we reviewed in Chapter 2, sentences like (1) were included in an experimental investigation conducted by Musolino (1998). In a Truth Value Judgment task, (1) was presented as a description of a context in which the detective had only succeeded in finding two of the four guys who participated in the story. The context employed by Musolino (1998) was designed to make (1) true on its adult (non-isomorphic) interpretation (i.e., the interpretation paraphrased in (2)), and false on its non-adult (isomorphic) interpretation (i.e., the interpretation paraphrased in (3)).

(2)   There are some guys that the detective didn't find.

(3)   It is not the case that the detective found some guys.

The finding was that children as old as 5;9 rejected the target sentences, whereas adults consistently accepted them. In particular, many of the children interviewed by Musolino (1998) pointed out that (1) was incorrect because the detective had indeed found some guys in the story. Apparently, children's rejection of (1) followed from an interpretation which is unavailable in the adult grammar, i.e., (3).

Before we consider Musolino's interpretation of the experimental findings, it is worth recalling another study on children's interpretation of indefinites in negative sentences. As reviewed in Chapter 2, Thornton (1994) investigated whether children are aware of the differences in meaning between questions like (4) and (5).

(4)   Didn't any of the turtles buy an apple?

(5)   Did any of the turtles not buy an apple?

The responses collected by Thornton (1994) show that children as young as 3;6 discriminated between the two questions. The findings by Thornton (1994) show that children younger than four responded "yes" in response to (4) and pointed to the turtles in the context that had bought an apple, whereas they responded "yes" in response to (5) but pointed to the turtles that had *not* bought an apple.

Taken together, previous research on children's interpretation of indefinites in negative sentences paints a conflicting picture. Children's interpretation of the indefinite *any* conforms to the adult grammar, but their interpretation of the indefinite *some* does not appear to reflect adult competence. In order to provide a unified description of children's interpretation of indefinites (in both their positive and negative version), Musolino (1998) and Musolino, Crain and Thornton (2000) proposed the Observation of Isomorphism. The Observation of Isomorphism states that "when syntactic scope and semantic scope do not coincide [for adults - *AG*], children's interpretations correlate with the interpretations determined by syntactic scope" (Musolino, 1998; p. 145).[2] Thus, the Observation of Isomorphism invoked by Musolino (1998) and Musolino, Crain and Thornton (2000) describes both children's non-adult interpretation of negative sentences containing the indefinite *some*, as well as their adult-like interpretation of questions containing the indefinite *any*.

The Observation of Isomorphism is invoked by Musolino (1998) to describe a richer set of facts than children's interpretation of indefinites in negative sentences. For example, Musolino (1998) also discovered that children's dependence on syntactic scope extends to their interpretation of negative sentences containing the universal quantifier *every*. Consider (6).

(6)   Every horse didn't jump over the fence.

In adult English, sentence (6) is ambiguous between the isomorphic reading paraphrased in (7)a and the non-isomorphic reading paraphrased in (8)a.[3]

(7)   a.   Every horse is such that it did not jump over the fence.
        b. $\forall(x) (\text{horse}(x) \rightarrow \neg \text{jumped over the fence}(x))$

---

2 As observed in Chapter 3, an interesting question raised by the Observation of Isomorphism is whether children's preference for the isomorphic interpretation of quantified sentences reflects a preference for the scope relations dictated by the linear order or a preference for scope relations dictated by the structural relationship between the relevant operators. This question was addressed by Lidz and Musolino (2002) who investigated the interpretation of sentences like *The smurf didn't catch two birds* by children learning English and Kannada, an SOV language where negation c-commands but follows the object noun. The conclusion reached by Lidz and Musolino (2002) is that, in assigning wide scope to negation, children exposed to either language adhere to structural conditions that are common to both English and Kannada.

3 See Carden (1973) for adults' interpretation of quantifiers in negative sentences and Kurtzman and MacDonald (1993) for adults' interpretation of multiple quantifiers.

(8)   a.   Not every horse is such that it jumped over the fence.

        b. $\neg\forall(x)$ (horse(x) $\rightarrow$ jumped over the fence(x))

Consistently with the findings about children's interpretation of the indefinite *some* in negative sentences, Musolino (1998) found that young children interpreted sentences like (6) on the isomorphic interpretation in (7)a. In short, children's interpretation of the universal quantifier *every* in negative sentences can be described by the Observation of Isomorphism, and their behavior is consistent with their interpretation of the indefinite *some* in negative sentences.

This chapter focuses on children's interpretation of *some* in negative sentences.[4] The present focus is motivated by three facts. First, children's interpretation of the positive polarity item *some* in negative sentences can be evaluated in light of the body of evidence about their knowledge of negative polarity items and related phenomena that has been extensively reviewed and expanded in the present study. Second, children's non-adult interpretation of negative sentences containing *every* can be described as a failure to access the interpretation that is preferred by adults. By contrast, under current assumptions, children's non adult-interpretation of *some* in negative sentences must be described as children's failure to access the only interpretation available to adults. Third, recent studies discussed by Musolino (2001) and Musolino and Lidz (2002b) suggest that young children can access the non-isomorphic interpretation of negative sentences containing the universal quantifier *every* in certain experimental conditions.[5] In light of these findings, children's interpretation of the indefinite *some* in the scope of negation stands out as the unresolved discrepancy between children's and adults' interpretation of quantifiers in negative sentences.

The difference in the interpretation of *some* and *any* in negative sentences is not the only difference between these two expressions. For present purposes, however, it is instructive to look at an analysis of *any* proposed by Kadmon and Landman, which emphasizes the similarities between *some* and *any*. The approach to the distribution and the interpretation of *any* proposed by Kadmon and Landman (1993) consists of three parts. First, *any* is treated as an indefinite. It is therefore expected to display the same kind of variability in its quantificational force revealed by all indefinites. Second, *any* is distinguished from other indefinites in that *any* widens the domain under consideration. Third,

---

4 We will discuss children's interpretation of negative sentences containing the universal quantifier *every* in the concluding section.

5 We will discuss these recent findings in the last section of the present chapter.

the use of *any* is subject to a semantic constraint, namely *any* "must STRENGTHEN the statement it occurs in, that is the semantic operation associated with it must create a stronger statement." [6] It is important to emphasize how the account proposed by Kadmon and Landman relates to the scope facts illustrated above. Kadmon and Landman (1993) argue that the negative polarity item *any* can be used instead of its positive polarity counterpart *some* in downward entailing contexts, because in downward entailing contexts the widening of the domain of quantification leads to a more informative statement. Thus, a cooperative speaker will use *any* in any downward entailing context, because the use of *any* will yield a more informative statement. Now, this does not mean that the plain indefinite *some* cannot occur in negative statements. More simply, the indefinite *some* can occur in a negative statement if some grammatical operation allows the indefinite noun phrase to be interpreted outside the scope of the negative operator. On this view, the interpretation of the indefinite *some* outside the scope of negation is closely related to the same properties that force the interpretation of the negative polarity item *any* in the scope of negation.[7]

The puzzle uncovered by Musolino is interesting for a second reason. Thus far we have highlighted the role of structure for language interpretation by young children. Importantly, we have argued that polarity phenomena are no exception to the structure dependent nature of linguistic operations. Taking disjunction as a case study, we reported experimental evidence showing that children's interpretation of *or* is sensitive to the environment in which it appears. For example, the interpretation of disjunction is affected by negation under the same structural constraints that are operative in the adult language. Similarly, the disjunction operator *or* is interpreted differently by children depending on whether it occurs in the first or in the second argument of the universal quantifier *every*. These considerations suggest that children are aware of the role of linguistic structure for grammatical operations. The findings documented by Musolino (1998) and Lidz and Musolino (2001), however, suggest that children's grammar might be constrained by linguistic structure to a greater extent than adults' grammar. Across natural languages, syntactic

---

6 Kadmon and Landman (1993; pp. 368-369, emphasis in text).

7 In a similar vein, Krifka (1995) argued that (the preference for) the wide-scope interpretation of *some* in negative sentences follows from the availability of the unambiguous sentence containing *any* as a possible way of conveying the same information expressed by the narrow-scope interpretation of *some*, i.e., the isomorphic interpretation.

structure determines what operations can and what operations cannot apply. However, most – if not all – natural languages make use of grammatical operations, either covert or overt, which alter the structure of the linguistic representation in a restricted number of ways. If the Observation of Isomorphism is correct, these operations are inaccessible to children.

It is pertinent to observe that the Observation of Isomorphism is not presented by Musolino (1998) as a learning principle. The Observation of Isomorphism is a descriptive generalization that can be derived from independently motivated properties of the Language Acquisition Device or from idiosyncratic properties of the particular quantifier involved. As a consequence, children's adherence to the isomorphic interpretation of sentences containing negation and a quantifier could in principle receive a different explanation for each quantifier. For instance, Musolino, Crain and Thornton (2000) derive children's initial stages in the interpretation of indefinites in the scope of negation as resulting from children's developing knowledge of the linguistic properties that distinguish between *some* and *any* and children's initial choice of more restricted grammars, i.e., grammars that license interpretations true in the narrowest set of circumstances (see Crain, Ni and Conway, 1994). They call this the Semantic Subset Principle.

An alternative account of children's interpretation of indefinites in negative sentences was proposed by Krämer (2000). Krämer (2000) reports new experimental findings showing that Dutch-speaking children also experience difficulties with indefinites in negative sentences. Importantly, however, the pattern of responses provided by Dutch-speaking children cannot be readily described by the Observation of Isomorphism. To account for the behavior of both English- and Dutch-speaking children, Krämer (2000) develops a novel account of children's interpretation of indefinites that draws upon the theory of indefinites proposed by van Geenhoven (1998). On Krämer's view, children only experience difficulty with the free variable interpretation of indefinites. More precisely, according to Krämer (2000), children resort to a predicative interpretation of indefinites, in circumstances where adults would adopt a free variable interpretation.

Despite the differences between the accounts proposed by Musolino, Crain and Thornton (2000) and Krämer (2000), these accounts share the assumption that children's behavior deserves a grammatical explanation. Musolino et al. (2000) and Krämer (2000) assume that the experimental findings show that children's and adults' grammars license different interpretations. In our view, this interpretation of the experimental findings is unwarranted, and so is the need for a grammatical explanation of the observed differences between child and adult grammars. In fact, just the opposite is true. Children and adults share the same grammar. What children and adults do not share is the ability to respond to experimental material that, we will argue, is infelicitous. This is the topic of the remainder of the chapter.

5.2 Empirical Problems for the Observation of Isomorphism

This section raises some empirical shortcomings of the Observation of Isomorphism. It bears repeating that the Observation of Isomorphism is offered simply as a descriptive generalization, and this is how we will consider it. We are not concerned with any specific grammatical proposal about children's interpretation of the indefinite *some* in the scope of negation. Both the account proposed by Musolino et al. (2000) and the one by Krämer (2000) would be plausible explanations of the apparent differences between child and adult grammars. What we doubt is whether there are any such differences. Let us now illustrate what aspects of children's behavior lead us to doubt the need for a grammatical explanation. We concentrate on the findings reported by Musolino (1998), because these findings are reported in great detail and because the experiments conducted by Musolino (1998) incorporate all the relevant features of experimental design (e.g., the Condition of Plausible Dissent discussed in Chapter 4).

As we have seen in Section 5.1, Musolino (1998) reports that 30 children (age: 3;10 to 6;6) unexpectedly rejected the target sentences 50% of the time. Each subject was presented with four target trials; the distribution of adult responses is plotted in Figure 1.

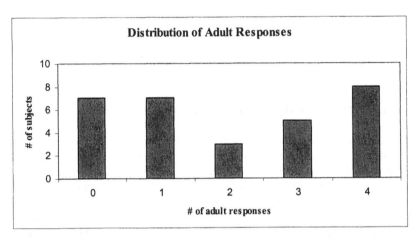

Figure 1 - Individual data from Experiment 3 – Musolino (1998)

These data can be described in two ways. As a first possibility, one could classify each subject on the basis of the response that she gave on *most* of the trials. This criterion of classification would lead us to count children as non-adults if they rejected the target sentences on at least three trials. Similarly, this criterion would lead us to classify as adults the children who accepted the target sentences on at least three trials. On this view, the data would yield a bimodal distribution, the effect of noise notwithstanding. As a second possibility, however, one could adopt a more fine-grained analysis and classify each subject on the basis of the response that she gave on *all* of the trials. This criterion would lead us to classify as non-adults only the children who rejected the target sentences on all four trials. Similarly, this criterion would lead us to classify as adults only the children who accepted the target sentences on all four trials. If one were to adopt this criterion, half of the subjects would not be assigned to either group. The question is which criterion one should adopt.

No experimental investigation is immune to experimental noise. But one needs to ask how much noise is reasonable to expect. This question is not simply resolved by assigning a numerical value. The question is ultimately resolved by discovering whether one would gain anything from the strictest classification (i.e., the classification that considers the responses that children gave on *all* trials). Noisy data are data which resist any theoretically relevant explanation. If one cannot find any explanation (or if we can only find explanations that lie outside the boundaries of the research question), then there is no point in engaging in statistical considerations. But if a pertinent explanation can be offered, then it is useful to scrutinize the data further.

As a first step into resolving this issue, one should determine whether all trials contribute equally to noise. A cursory look at the data reported by Musolino (1998) shows that this is not the case. Let us first consider the seven subjects who only provided one adult response. These subjects never produced the adult response for the fourth experimental trial (see below). Now, consider the five subjects who provided three adult responses (or one non-adult response). By looking at the data, one can observe that four of these subjects gave that non-adult response on the same experimental trial, the fourth experimental trial. This pattern of behavior is unlikely to arise by accident, so it invites us to further examine the offending trial.

Ordinarily, nobody would object to the criterion adopted by Musolino (1998) and Musolino et al. (2000), who classify each subject depending on the responses that she gave on *most* trials. However, the present case would seem to call for a stricter criterion. If one adopts a stricter criterion, classifying each subject on the basis of the response that she gave on all the trials, then two further observations can be made. First, fifteen children accessed both the isomorphic and the non-isomorphic reading. Second, the conclusion that children only access the isomorphic reading is based on the responses provided by 7 children, less than one fourth of the child subjects.

To illustrate our point, consider two trials from Experiment 3 in Musolino (1998) in further detail. On the fourth experimental trial in that experiment, children were told a story about an old man and four friends at a barbecue. When the barbecue was over, the old man decided to mow the lawn. While he was mowing the lawn he accidentally hurt two of his guests, though two other men remained unscathed. At the end of the story, children were presented with the sentence in (9).

(9)   The old man didn't hurt some guys.

This trial can be contrasted with the one in which the story was about a detective playing hide-and-seek with his four friends. As we saw in Section 5.1, the detective found two guys, but he failed to find the other two. Children were asked to evaluate the following sentence:

(10)   The detective didn't find some guys.

Despite the similarity of the story, the two trials yielded a different response pattern from children. In particular, the thirty children interviewed by Musolino (1998) rejected the target sentences in (9) 20 times (67%) and they rejected the sentence in (10) 12 times (40%). Among all the trials of the experiment, (10) gave rise to the lowest number of non-adult responses, whereas (9) yielded the highest number of non-adult responses.

Regardless of the significance of the different percentages of rejections, in the statistical sense, this pattern calls for further consideration. If one respects all the features of experimental design, as Musolino (1998) did, the results should yield a clearer pattern than the one that was observed (see Crain and Thornton, 1999; Thornton and Wexler, 1999). Whenever such behavioral patterns arise, the research strategy should be to determine if there is some particular factor of the study which is responsible for the particular reading that is accessed in each experimental trial. We pursue this hypothesis in the next section, where we argue that previous research has failed to control for the felicity of the linguistic materials. Some trials were felicitous, but other trials were not. Children performed accordingly, i.e., they performed better on felicitous trials than on infelicitous ones. This interpretation of the findings rests on the assumption that children are sensitive to the satisfaction of felicity conditions, and this is the source of much current debate, as acknowledged in Chapter 4. Thus, we would like to recall the relevant evidence in favor of this assumption.

5.3 Children and Felicity Conditions

The role of felicity conditions in language comprehension has received an increasing amount of attention in the last decade. In this section, we focus on some empirical evidence showing that (a) children's linguistic competence can be obscured by experiments that do not satisfy the felicity conditions associated with the target sentences, and that (b) children's responses to infelicitous experimental stimuli are not limited to the acceptance of the target sentences, but can also take the form of 'motivated rejections' of the target sentences.

The role of felicity conditions associated with specific linguistic constructions in child language can be illustrated by children's interpretation of temporal conjunctions. In several studies, children were reported to be more successful in acting out the request in (11) than the one in (12) (see Clark, 1971; Amidon and Carey, 1972).

(11)   After you push the car, push the truck.

(12)   Before you push the car, push the truck.

Children's behavior was often interpreted as reflecting a difficulty in interpreting temporal conjunctions, especially when the order of mention does not match the order with which the events should take place (i.e., (12)). Crain (1982) focused on a different source of children's errors. In particular, Crain (1982) pointed out that both (11) and (12) *presuppose* that the child intends to push the car, and these sentences *assert* that there is an additional activity the child should perform before or after pushing the car. The presupposition was not satisfied in the experimental context, however, because it had not been established that the child was going to push the car. Thus, Crain (1982) argued that children's behavior reflects a difficulty in accommodating the presuppositions triggered by both sentences (11) and (12), rather than any difficulty with the subordinating temporal conjunctions.[8] Consistent with this hypothesis, Crain showed that children's 'errors' were significantly reduced once the relevant presupposition was satisfied.

In light of this and many similar findings, we can now focus on the particular response documented by previous studies of children's interpretation of negative sentences. It is reasonable to assume that confusion leads children (or anyone) to over-accept the target sentences (see Grimshaw and Rosen, 1990). Against this background, it is hard to see how children's *rejection* of the target sentences in the Musolino study could result from the violation of a felicity condition. Children's ability to motivate their rejection of the target sentences might be viewed as an additional difficulty for the claim that a felicity condition is at issue. Nevertheless, recent studies on children's interpretation of universally quantified sentences show that children can produce a pattern of motivated non-adult rejection (of experimental stimuli) as a result of the infelicity of the task.

The relevant study was presented in Chapter 4. One of the most discussed findings of research on children's understanding of the universal quantifier *every* is that preschool, and even school age children, reject a sentence like (13) in a context in which three boys are each riding an elephant and there is an additional elephant that is not ridden by anybody (see Inhelder and Piaget, 1964).

(13)   Every boy is riding an elephant.

---

8 See Lewis (1979) for discussion of accommodation.

To justify their rejection of (13), children often point to the extra object, i.e., the elephant that is not being ridden by any boy. As we saw, accounts of children's non-adult responses can be divided into ones that attribute children's responses to deviant linguistic analyses of the universal quantifier *every*, and ones that attribute them to non-grammatical factors. Among the non-grammatical accounts, Crain, Thornton, Boster, Conway, Lillo-Martin and Woodams (1996) maintained that the contexts employed in previous research did not allow the subject to conceive an alternative scenario that would make the sentence false, a felicity condition for judgments of truth. The sentence in (13) becomes felicitous if, for example, some boy at least considered riding some animal besides an elephant. In experimental contexts that make this possible outcome available to children, the non-adult responses documented in previous studies disappear.

To recap, we have reviewed two representative studies highlighting children's sensitivity to felicity conditions. In light of these studies, it becomes important to determine whether anything of this sort might be at issue in experiments assessing children's interpretation of indefinites in negative sentences.

5.4 Negation and Felicity Conditions

Negative sentences constitute a rich domain of linguistic research. Drawing upon the principles of pragmatic theory, numerous psycholinguists have also focused on the felicity conditions associated with the use of negative sentences. We can introduce the role of felicity conditions in interpreting negative sentences through the example in (14), due to Wason (1972).

(14)   5 is not an even number.

The sentence in (14) is true. Still, (14) appears to be more difficult for people to process than a positive sentence like (15), although both (14) and (15) seem to express the same proposition.

(15)   5 is an odd number.

Interestingly, the difficulty associated with (14) is considerably mitigated if that sentence is preceded by a positive statement, as in (16).

(16)   4 is an even number, and/but 5 is not an even number.

The difficulty associated with negative sentences was also discussed by De Villiers and Tager Flusberg (1975). Consider (17).

(17)   I didn't drive to work.

As pointed out by De Villiers and Tager Flusberg (1975), the statement in (17) "is more plausible, and consequently easier to comprehend, if it is made by someone who normally drives rather than by someone who commutes by train" (p. 279). According to De Villiers and Tager Flusberg (1975), this property of negative sentences results from the fact that "negative statements are generally used to point out discrepancies between a listener's presumed expectations and the facts" (p. 279) (see also Wason, 1965 and Givon, 1978).

The observation that negative sentences are subject to a specific set of felicity conditions led De Villiers and Tager Flusberg (1975) to an experimental investigation of children's comprehension of negation. In the experiment, children were asked to complete negative questions (i.e., "This is not a ___?") in contexts in which the use of a negative sentence was or was not plausible (e.g., in the plausible context, the experimenter had pointed to various instances of a particular object before pointing to a different object). The results showed that children as young as two respond significantly faster when the negative question is presented in the plausible context. De Villiers and Tager Flusberg (1975) interpret this finding as evidence that very young children know that the use of negative sentences is subject to the satisfaction of specific felicity conditions.

A similar conclusion for adult subjects was reached by Glenberg, Robertson, Jansen and Johnson-Glenberg (1999). These researchers conducted three experiments investigating adults' difficulty in interpreting negative sentences. In one of the experiments, the subjects were asked to read negative sentences in contexts that supported the positive expectation triggered by the negative sentence and in contexts that did not support this expectation. The finding was that "when negated sentences are used in an appropriate context, readers do not take longer to understand them" (Glenberg et al., 1999; p. 19). According to Glenberg et al. (1999), the experimental findings support the conclusion that "difficulty with negation is demonstrated to be an artifact of presentation out of context" (Glenberg et al., 1999; p. 19).

We have reviewed previous studies with children and adult subjects investigating the difficulty of negative sentences. The findings show that subjects experience a difficulty in processing negative sentences in the absence of context, and in contexts that are arguably infelicitous for their use. The findings, however, suggest that the difficulty associated with negative sentences can be mitigated if the target sentence is preceded by a positive lead-in or used to point out that an expectation went unfulfilled.

The exact 'nature' of the difficulty associated with negative sentences remains to be determined, however. This issue was discussed extensively by Horn (1989), who argued that the facts above do not highlight a property of negative sentences per se; rather, they reflect a consequence of the way negative sentences are ordinarily used. In order to support his claim, Horn (1989) shows how the infelicity of negative sentences in ordinary contexts can be explained by the interplay of pragmatic principles.

In our view, the arguments presented in Horn (1989) underscore the pragmatic nature of the phenomenon under investigation. For the purposes of the experimentalist, however, this should not undermine the importance of the phenomenon itself. Whether it is a semantic or a pragmatic phenomenon, the difficulty of negative sentences needs to be taken into account in the experimental set up. In short, experimental studies using negative sentences with child or adult subjects should ensure that subjects' responses are not vitiated by the infelicitous use of the target sentences.

In light of the conflicting findings documented in previous research on children's interpretation of indefinites in negative sentences, it becomes important to ask whether the felicity conditions associated with negative sentences were satisfied in the studies that evoked non-adult responses from children. With this goal in mind, let us return to the trials employed by Musolino (1998). As we mentioned, on one experimental trial children were told a story about five friends at a barbecue. When the barbecue was over, the old man decided to mow the lawn and accidentally hurt two of his guests. At the end of the story, children were presented with the sentence in (18).

(18)   The old man didn't hurt some guys.

The question is whether (18) is a felicitous statement in the context under consideration. The context does not provide any reason why the old man could have been expected to hurt his friends. In absence of any explicit expectation about the old man's behavior, children were left with their own expectations about real life. Even a four year old probably knows that one is not expected to run over his friends with a lawnmower. If so, then the test sentence in (18) is infelicitous, because it does not point out a discrepancy between the final outcome and an expectation that is established by the story, or by real world knowledge. In fact, if children were to appeal to their knowledge about the real world, they would probably expect the old man *not* to hurt any of the guys. The sentence in (18) would provide a felicitous utterance in a context in which it was established that the old man was likely to hurt all of his friends. Out of this context, however, the story we just considered represents a likely candidate for a non-felicitous use of a negative sentence.

Compare this with Story 1 in the Musolino study. This story was about the detective who was playing hide and seek with some of his friends. In this story the detective found two guys, but failed to find the remaining two. Children were then asked to evaluate the following sentence.

(19)   The detective didn't find some guys.

Is (19) felicitous in the context under consideration? The answer is not clear. The story did not establish the expectation that the detective would find all the guys. However, this is an assumption that a typical 5 year old who ever played hide and seek *could* make.[9]

In short, although neither trial explicitly built up an expectation as to what the main character would do, real world knowledge could have made different contributions on the two trials. Could this be enough to prompt children's correct interpretation of the target sentence? By looking at the data reported by Musolino (1998), it is apparent that real world knowledge does not suffice to yield an adult pattern, but it *does* produce an effect. Recall, Story 1 gave rise to the lowest number of non-adult responses, whereas Story 4 yielded the highest number of non-adult responses. This difference is consistent with our speculation on children's use of real world knowledge to accommodate the infelicity of the target sentence.

To recap, linguists and psycholinguists have investigated the differences between affirmative and negative statements with respect to ambiguity and felicity. We have argued that the felicity conditions associated with negative sentences must be incorporated into the experimental design of studies assessing children's linguistic competence, and we have claimed that the failure to do so might be at the origin of previous findings about children's interpretation of indefinites. The difference between different trials in previous experimental studies is consistent with the hypothesis that previous studies failed to control for the felicity of the linguistic material. The next section presents the findings

---

9 Although it is reasonable that a typical five year old would know that when playing hide and seek all the characters have to be found, it is less clear whether every child would take this knowledge to be relevant for the task.

of an experiment designed to seek more robust evidence in favor of this hypothesis.

5.5 Experimental Design

5.5.1 Experiment V

This section presents the findings of an experiment employing the Truth Value Judgment task (Crain and McKee, 1985; Crain and Thornton, 1998). As we observed in Chapter 2, the optimal design of the Truth Value Judgment task requires a context that falsifies the adult interpretation of the target sentence and verifies the non-adult interpretation under investigation. As discussed by Musolino (1998), however, this ideal state of affairs cannot be obtained in the present case, since the non-isomorphic reading of (20) is true in a superset of the circumstances that make (20) true on the isomorphic reading.[10]

(20)   The detective didn't find some guys.

Given this state of affairs and the desire to minimize the differences between our experiment and previous studies, the present experiment employed the same design as Experiment 3 in Musolino (1998): the context makes the isomorphic reading false and the non-isomorphic reading true.

To investigate the role of felicity conditions in children's interpretation of negative sentences, we manipulated children's expectations about the final outcome of the story (see below). Thirty children participated in the experiment, divided in two groups. One group of 15 children (Group I, age: 4;01 to 5;06 – mean age: 4;10) was asked to evaluate negative sentences that truthfully described the final outcome of the story and expressed a mismatch between the final outcome and the expectation built during the story. The second group of 15 children (Group II, age: 4;02 to 5;8 – mean age: 4;11) was asked to evaluate

---

10 If the detective did not find any guys, then it is also true that there are some guys that the detective did not find, but not vice versa. More generally, if a sentence like (20) is true on its isomorphic interpretation, that sentence is also true on its non-isomorphic interpretation, but not vice versa. To distinguish between the two readings, then, one can only consider a situation in which the non-isomorphic interpretation is true but the isomorphic interpretation is false.

negative sentences that also truthfully described the final outcome of the story, but ones that failed to express a mismatch between the final outcome and the expectation built during the story. Each group of children was presented with four target trials, preceded by one warm-up trial and interspersed with three filler trials to balance the number of 'yes' and 'no' responses.

Let us illustrate the experimental design using a typical trial. Consider the trial in (21), which is a modified version of Story 1 of Experiment 3 conducted by Musolino (1998).

(21)   "This is a story about a firefighter who is going to play hide and seek with four dwarves. While the firefighter counts, the dwarves look for a spot to hide. When the firefighter has finished counting, he starts looking for the dwarves. Initially, the firefighter cannot find any of the dwarves and he is ready to give up, but then he decides to try harder. He finds one dwarf who was hiding behind a barrel and he asks the dwarf: "Ok, am I done now?" and the dwarf says: "No! there are three more dwarves for you to find." The firefighter spots a second dwarf who was hiding inside the barrel, and he asks him: "Ok, am I done now?" but the dwarf says: "No! there are two more dwarves for you to find." The firefighter starts looking again, but then he says: "Those two dwarves did a very good job, I cannot find them. I give up"."

At this point one group of children was presented with the sentence in (22) and the second group was asked to evaluate (23).

(22)   This was a story about a firefighter playing hide and seek with four dwarves and I know what happened. <u>The firefighter didn't find some dwarves.</u>

(23)   This was a story about a firefighter playing hide and seek with four dwarves and I know what happened. <u>The firefighter didn't miss some dwarves.</u>

Before we report the results, let us consider the extent to which the two target sentences differ. The target sentences in (22) and (23) do not differ in truth value, since both sentences are true in the scenario under consideration. In particular, (22) is true because there are two dwarves that the firefighter did not find, and (23) is true because there are two dwarves that the firefighter did not miss, namely the dwarves that he found. The two sentences differ with respect to their felicity, however.

The story conveys the expectation that the firefighter would find all the dwarves, but it does not build up the expectation that the firefighter would miss all of them. As a consequence, (22) is felicitous because it expresses a mismatch between what happened and what was expected to happen (i.e., the number of dwarves that the firefighter found and the number of dwarves that he was expected to find). By contrast, (23) is infelicitous because there is no immediate mismatch between what happened and what was expected to happen (i.e., the number of dwarves that the firefighter missed and the number of dwarves that he was supposed to find). This simply follows from the lack of any expectation that the firefighter would miss all the dwarves. As a consequence of this difference, the experimental hypothesis was that children would respond in a fully adult-like fashion to sentences like (22), and that possible non-adult responses would be limited to ones like (23).

This is exactly what we found. Children accepted sentences like (22) on 54 out of 60 trials (90%), and they accepted sentences like (23) only on 30 out of 60 trials (50%) (see the Appendix for experimental details). The difference between the two conditions is deeper than the numbers suggest, however. In order to further assess children's judgments, children were occasionally asked to motivate their answers by pointing to the characters that "made Kermit right." Interestingly, when children accepted sentences like (22), they consistently pointed out that the puppet was right because the firefighter had failed to find two of the dwarves. By contrast, some of the children who gave adult responses to (23) could not motivate their answers: in particular, they did not point to the dwarves that the firefighter had not missed, i.e., the dwarves that the firefighter had found. In our view, these children's grammatical competence was obscured because of the infelicity of the linguistic material, and it is possible that they accepted the target sentence without accessing its adult interpretation (see Grimshaw and Rosen, 1990).

Thirty-six native speakers of English participated as adult controls in a video-taped version of the experiment. Twenty-two subjects accepted sentences like (22) in 66 out of 86 trials (77%), and the remaining fourteen subjects accepted sentences like (23) only in 27 out of 56 trials (48%).

Before we consider the relevance of the present findings, it is important to comment on the linguistic materials; in particular, the use of sentences like (23). The reader might object that the meaning of the verb *miss* has some negative component to it. Thus, at some abstract level, an increase in processing cost might be associated with such sentences, caused by the presence of negation and a negative-like verb.[11] In our view this objection is irrelevant. First, the focus of our research has been on the conditions under which children's linguistic competence emerges in the experimental setting, rather than on the conditions under which such competence is obscured. Second, if our hypothesis is on the right track, the verb *hurt* used in the Musolino study yields the same effect as the verb *miss* in our experiment, although the former does not seem to share the negative flavor of the latter. Third, we believe it should be possible to 'impair' children's competence without changing the verb used in the experiment. For example, imagine a context in which an archer is trying to hit four targets, each one held by a different man. Now, suppose that the archer hits two of the four targets, but misses the remaining two and accidentally hits the men holding those two targets. Now consider the sentences below.

(24)   The archer didn't hit some <u>targets</u>.

(25)   The archer didn't hit some <u>men</u>.

Intuitively, (24) is more felicitous than (25), despite the fact that the same verb occurs in the two sentences. This difference is consistent with our hypothesis: (24), but not (25), felicitously points out a contrast between the context under consideration and the expectation that the archer hit all the targets.

5.6 Conclusion

The experimental findings reported in the present chapter reveal children's adult-like interpretation of negative sentences containing the indefinite *some* when the felicity conditions associated with the target sentences are satisfied. In light of these results, the differences observed in previous research between children's interpretation of the positive polarity item *some* and the negative polarity item *any* can be reconciled. The reader might view the main point of the present chapter as methodological in nature. However, as Crain and Wexler observe "methodology is intertwined with theory in nontrivial ways" (Crain and Wexler, 1999; p. 387). The present study attempted to develop experimental methodology as prescribed by *research* methodology.

---

11 The same objection could be extended to two additional trials of the experiment (see the Appendix).

The present chapter focused on one specific aspect of the difference between children's and adults' interpretation of negative sentences. In particular, it focused on children's and adults' interpretation of negative sentences containing the indefinite *some*. This was a pretext, however. Our goal was not to adjudicate between alternative explanations of children's non-adult interpretation of *some* in negative sentences. Our goal was to determine whether children's non-adult interpretation of *some* in negative sentences, which has been documented in previous research, calls for a grammatical explanation. We have argued against such a conclusion. Furthermore, we have credited 4-year-olds with full knowledge of the grammatical properties of the indefinite *some*, as well as knowledge of the pragmatic conditions that govern its use in negative sentences.[12] This does not exclude the possibility that children might fail to distinguish between *some* and *any* at earlier stages of language development. Our results, however, show that it would be unwarranted to argue that 4-year-olds have incomplete knowledge of the linguistic properties of *some* and, more importantly, that it would be unwarranted to argue that children's interpretation of *some* in negative sentences is entirely dictated by syntactic scope.

The interpretive properties of lexical items like *some* and *any* are subject to cross-linguistic variation. Therefore, it would not be surprising if child language turned out to differ from adult language in this respect. However, it would be surprising if semantic scope in child language turned out to be securely tied to syntactic scope, since most (if not all) natural languages make available covert operations that affect syntactic scope (for similar remarks see also Musolino and Lidz, 2002b).

Within the context of the present study, the experimental findings bear additional relevance. In Chapter 3, we repeatedly argued that children do not entertain structure independent hypotheses. This conclusion was based on two kinds of results. First, children do not apply the relevant De Morgan's law when

---

12 Strictly speaking, we have showed that children can access the non-isomorphic interpretation of the sentences under consideration but we cannot argue that this is the only possible interpretation. This might not be an unwelcome consequence of the findings, however. In fact, it is not entirely clear whether the isomorphic interpretation of *some* in the scope of negation is completely unavailable to adults (see the responses of the adult controls who participated in the experiment). One logical possibility would be to investigate children's interpretation of sentences like *The firefighter didn't find some guys* in a context in which the firefighter did not find any of the guys, although such an experiment would have to take into account the differences between children's and adults' readiness to compute scalar implicatures (see Gualmini, 2001).

or is preceded but not c-commanded by negation. Second, children *do* apply the relevant De Morgan's law when *or* is preceded and c-commanded by negation. This last finding was unanticipated from a pre-theoretical point of view. Focusing on children's correct interpretation of *or* in the scope of negation, however, the results would look less surprising in light of the Observation of Isomorphism. If children's interpretation is constrained by surface structure, one might argue that their application of the relevant De Morgan's law simply followed from their inability to disregard the scope relations dictated by surface syntax. The findings reported in the present chapter show that this was not the case. The findings show that children's interpretation of scope-bearing elements is not constrained by surface scope any more than adults' interpretation is. Thus, children's interpretation of *or* in the scope of negation, as documented in Chapter 3, is indeed surprising from a pre-theoretical point of view.

The experimental findings reported above have further implications for the account proposed by Krämer (2000). First, the experimental design employed by Krämer (2000) did not satisfy the felicity conditions associated with negative sentences. Assuming that the pattern of responses documented by Krämer (2000) would fail to emerge in experiments that satisfied those felicity conditions, a grammatical account of Dutch-speaking children's non-adult responses is unwarranted. Until evidence to the contrary is provided, we feel secure in continuing to accept the null hypothesis that English- and Dutch-speaking children's difficulty with negative sentences should receive the same explanation. [13] It should be noted, moreover, that the claim that children's difficulty is due to the failure to satisfy the felicity conditions associated with negative sentences does not make any prediction about *how* children should respond to infelicitous test sentences. Thus, Krämer's observation that Dutch-speaking children's responses did not conform to the Observation of Isomorphism (or to the structural relationship dictated by c-command) is perfectly compatible with the present proposal.

To end, we wish to qualify our interpretation of the experimental findings. The focus of the present chapter has been on the experimental features that possibly make felicitous the use of negative statements. This no doubt relates to the experimental features that possibly make the use of negative statements *infelicitous*. Our particular way of making negative sentences felicitous (or infelicitous) should not distract the reader from the main concern of this chapter,

---

13 Of course, this reasoning assumes that English and Dutch indefinites do not differ in any relevant respect.

namely how children interpret negative sentences when they are used in felicitous contexts.

A growing body of evidence suggests that the felicity of negative sentences can also be attained if the negative sentence is preceded by a positive lead-in. For example, in Chapter 2 we argued that this factor facilitates children's comprehension of sentences containing the quantified expression *None of the Ns* (e.g., *none of the pirates*). A similar interpretation applies to more recent findings about the interpretation of the universal quantifier *every* in negative sentences.

In a series of experimental investigations, Musolino and Lidz (2002b) showed that the use of a positive lead-in dramatically improves children's performance with negative sentences containing the universal quantifier. Recall that Musolino (1998) reported that children's adherence to syntactic scope extends to their interpretation of negative sentences containing the universal quantifier *every*. In particular, Musolino (1998) found that young children's preferred interpretation for sentences like (26) was the isomorphic interpretation in (27)a.

(26)   Every horse didn't jump over the fence.

(27)   a.   Every horse is such that it did not jump over the fence.
        b. $\forall(x)$ (horse(x) $\rightarrow$ $\neg$ jumped over the fence(x))

Interestingly, Musolino and Lidz (2002b) showed that the use of a positive lead-in as in (28) leads children to access the non-isomorphic interpretation of the target sentence.

(28)   Every horse jumped over the log and/but <u>every horse didn't jump over the fence</u>.

The use of positive lead-ins constitutes an additional tool for the experimentalist. But this fact is by no means at odds with the claim defended in this chapter. Further research will address the extent to which the infelicity of different negative sentences can be mitigated by different alterations of the context. First, one needs to determine why each contextual manipulation has the particular effect that it has. Second, one needs to determine why the *failure* to perform any contextual manipulation has the particular effect that it has (i.e., why children resort to the isomorphic interpretation of the target sentence).

As to why each contextual manipulation has the particular effect that it has, it is worth examining the role of the contextual manipulation performed in our own experiment. Recall that on a typical trial, children were told a story about a firefighter playing hide and seek with four dwarves. At the end of the story, the firefighter succeeded in finding two dwarves, but failed to find the remaining two. The contextual manipulation consisted in pointing out repeatedly that the firefighter was expected to find all the dwarves. Thus, the contextual manipulation conveyed the expectation that the story would culminate in the event described in (29) and more formally in (30).

(29)   The firefighter found every dwarf.

(30) $\forall$(x) (dwarf(x) $\rightarrow$ the firefighter found (x))

Now, the negation of the prospected outcome (i.e., the negation of (29)) can be represented as in (31) or equivalently as in (32).

(31) $\neg\forall$(x) (dwarf(x) $\rightarrow$ the firefighter found (x))

(32) $\exists$(x) (dwarf(x) & $\neg$ the firefighter found (x))

It is pertinent to observe that (32) mirrors the interpretation of the target sentence under investigation, reported below as (33).

(33)   The firefighter didn't find some dwarves.

These observations are highly speculative, but they suggest that the children we interviewed accessed the wide scope reading of the indefinite *some* over negation because this interpretation closely mirrored the negation of the outcome projected by the story. This suggests that the contextual manipulation we performed had the particular effect that it had because (a) the expectation was a proposition about *all* the dwarves having a certain property and (b) the target sentence expressed a proposition about some dwarves not having that property. The felicity of the target sentence results from the combination of these two factors. Speculative as these remarks may be, they suggest that the felicity of the target sentence would not be reached if (a) the expectation was not a proposition about all the dwarves having a certain property (e.g., if the firefighter only had to find two dwarves) or (b) the target sentence did not express a proposition about some dwarves not having that property (e.g., the target sentence in (23), *The firefighter didn't miss some dwarves*). It is important to observe that, on this view, the success of our specific contextual manipulation is intimately connected with the logical form under investigation.[14]

Now we turn to the contextual manipulation performed by Musolino and Lidz (2002b). Recall that these researchers showed that children can access the non-isomorphic interpretation of sentences containing the universal quantifier and negation when the target sentence is preceded by a positive lead-in, as in (34).

(34)   Every horse jumped over the log and/but <u>every horse didn't jump over the fence</u>.

In order to explain children's improved performance with sentences like (34), we could simply assume that (34) is a felicitous sentence and then ask why children interpret felicitous sentences in the particular way that they do. One possibility is that, when the sentence is felicitous, children access the interpretation that makes the sentence true in the widest range of circumstances.

In a study about children's and adults' interpretation of sentences containing the focus operator *only*, Crain et al. (1994) tried to tease apart the different role of the parser and the Language Acquisition Device (LAD). According to Crain et al. (1994), the LAD responds to demands of learnability. In particular, the LAD must constrain children's hypothesis space so that children initially interpret any given sentence in its most restricted interpretation. Thus, for any sentence that is ambiguous for adults, the LAD initially leads children to adopt the interpretation that makes the sentence true in the most restricted set of circumstances. This is the Semantic Subset Principle

---

14 An alternative logical form could be facilitated by the same expectation. This is the non-isomorphic interpretation of sentences containing the universal quantifier and negation, which would mirror (31). It is pertinent to observe, however, that children's interpretation of this kind of sentences (e.g., *Every horse didn't jump over the fence*) might derive from a different source. As we reported in Chapter 2, children as old as 5 tend to rephrase a sentence like *None of the pirates found the jewel or the necklace* as *Every pirate didn't find the jewel or the necklace*. We did not offer any explanation for this aspect of children's behavior. However, given that children rephrase an unambiguous sentence through an ambiguous one, it is possible that they would preserve the similarity between the two sentences by preferring to a great extent the interpretation of *Every pirate didn't find the jewel or the necklace* that also constitutes a possible logical form for *None of the pirates found the jewel or the necklace*, namely the isomorphic interpretation.

mentioned in Section 5.2. When children acquire an additional meaning, however, their interpretation is not subject to demands of learnability anymore. According to Crain et al., the parser now guides children in the same way it guides adults, leading them to "construct a mental representation of a situation that is consistent with each of the alternative interpretations of the sentence".[15] In other words, when the acquisition process is complete, the parser will lead children to interpret ambiguous sentences on their less restricted interpretation. Notice that this explanation does not hinge upon the particular positive lead-in used in (34). By inference, this explanation does not call for any constraint on what positive sentence would make felicitous a negative sentence.[16]

Let us now consider why children respond to the failure to satisfy the relevant felicity conditions in the particular way that they do. One possibility discussed by Musolino (1998) draws on the fact that children show a preference for the interpretation of the target sentence that makes the sentence true in the most restricted set of circumstances (see Crain et al., 1994). On the particular view advocated in this chapter, one could argue that children respond to the infelicity of the target sentence by being conservative. Importantly, the choice of the most restrictive interpretation would allow children to revise their hypothesis, if needed, on the basis of positive evidence. Crain et al. (1994) were concerned with the language acquisition process. Our results show that in the present case both relevant readings are available to children, and this makes the properties of the Language Acquisition Device irrelevant. Thus, one would have to modify Crain et al.'s proposal to yield the same results (selecting the most restricted interpretation) when sentences are infelicitous.[17] On this view, children would select the most restricted interpretation because that interpretation can be falsified more easily.

A second alternative draws upon the relationship between the interpretation accessed by children and the relevant expectation. Consider the sentence in (35), and the two alternative logical forms in (36).

(35)   The firefighter didn't miss some dwarves.

---

15 Crain et al. (1994; p. 449)

16 Musolino (2001) discusses empirical evidence that suggests that (a) only a limited class of positive lead-ins mitigate the infelicity of the negative sentence or that (b) only some negative sentences are made felicitous by a positive lead-in.

17 This solution would not be entirely consistent with the proposal advanced by Crain et al., whose main purpose was to highlight the *differences* between the Language Acquisition Device and the parser.

(36)   a.   ∃(x) (dwarf(x) & ¬ the firefighter miss (x))
         b.   ¬∃(x) (dwarf(x) & the firefighter miss (x))

We hypothesized that (35) is felicitous on the relevant scope-assignment (i.e., (36)a) if the context supports the expectation that the firefighter would miss all of the dwarves. Similarly, one could claim that (35) tends to be interpreted on the narrow scope reading (i.e., (36)b), if the context supports the expectation that the firefighter would miss *some* – and potentially not all – of the dwarves. Now, neither expectation was supported in our experimental context, because the firefighter was expected to miss none of the dwarves. Thus, children had to modify their own expectations about the context, in a way that would make the sentence felicitous on some reading. Children had to choose between modifying their expectation in a way that (a) the firefighter would have to miss *some* of the dwarves or that (b) the firefighter would have to miss *all* of the dwarves. Crucially, the latter option would entail the former. Thus, at some level of abstraction, the expectation that the firefighter would miss some of the dwarves would arise anyway. Modifying the context only to accommodate this expectation while remaining neutral as to whether the firefighter would miss all of the dwarves amounts to a *minimal* modification of the subject's expectations.[18]

Speculative as they may be, these observations should remind the reader of the Principle of Parsimony, proposed by Crain and Steedman (1985; p. 333)

> "If there is a reading that carries fewer unsatisfied but consistent presuppositions or entailments that any other, then, other criteria of plausibility being equal, that reading will be adopted as most plausible by the hearer, and the presuppositions in question will be incorporated in his or her model."

In the present case, the child might attempt to modify her own *expectations* about the context in a way that closely resembles the scenario prescribed by the Principle of Parsimony. On this account, children access the isomorphic interpretation of indefinites in negative sentences because that interpretation allows them to modify their expectation about the context as conservatively as possible. It bears observing that, on this view, the fact that children resort to the isomorphic interpretation of negative sentences has nothing to do with principles of grammar. As far as grammar is concerned, both the narrow scope and the wide scope interpretation of indefinites in negative sentences are available to

---

18 Of course, real world knowledge might also play a role here.

children, and the selection between the two interpretations depends on mechanisms that do not reside within the grammar module.

A final comment should be made about the relevance of the present findings for current research in language acquisition. As we acknowledged in Section 5.2, Musolino (1998) presented the Observation of Isomorphism as a descriptive generalization. The Observation of Isomorphism described what was common to children's interpretation of a variety of quantifiers in negative sentences. On this view, a different aspect of children's developing linguistic knowledge might explain children's resorting to syntactic scope as the origin of semantic scope for all the quantifiers under consideration. This grammatical view has been recently challenged by Musolino (2001) on the basis of more recent experiments assessing children's interpretation of the universal quantifier *every* in negative sentences (see above). The findings, Musolino (2001) argues, suggest that the grammatical view of children's non-adult responses to negative sentences is unwarranted in that they show that children can access the non-isomorphic interpretation of negative sentences as a result of contextual manipulation.

On the basis of these more recent findings, Musolino (2001) attributes children's non-adult responses to their developing performance system.[19] The research reported in the present paper apparently supports this conclusion, in that it shows how contextual manipulations lead children to access the non-isomorphic interpretation of negative sentences containing the indefinite *some*. However, our interpretation of the findings is different from the one offered by Musolino (2001). Musolino's conclusion fails to recognize that the contextual manipulation that leads to children's improved performance with negative sentences also leads to *adults'* improved performance with negative sentences. If anything, the present findings as well as the ones documented in Musolino and Lidz (2002b) show that children and adults share the same performance system as well as the same linguistic competence (see Pinker, 1984; Crain and Thornton, 1998). What children and adults do not necessarily share is the ability to accommodate experimental stimuli that violate any conditions on the felicitous use of linguistic expressions.

The present findings also highlight children's pragmatic competence in that they reveal children's ability to carry out the pragmatic inferencing that leads to the non-isomorphic interpretation of *some* in negative sentences. As a consequence, the findings cast doubts on much current research on children's pragmatic competence (see Gualmini, 2001 for a review and a different view that draws upon the similarities between children and adults). Further research is

---

19 See also Musolino and Lidz (2002a).

needed to determine how the present findings might help in evaluating current models of children's pragmatic competence.

Finally, the present research extends a line of inquiry originally proposed by Crain and Steedman (1985). In a study on adults' interpretation of relative clauses, these researchers focused on the importance of context in language comprehension. Importantly, they argued that there really is no null context. If the experimenter presents the subject with sentences in absence of context, then the subject will mentally come up with one. Similarly, our study shows that there is no null expectation about how a context should be described. Some contexts are more likely to be described by a negative sentence than other contexts. If a negative sentence is used in a context for which subjects do not expect a negative sentence, they might revise their expectations about the context in a way that makes the negative sentence appropriate. It is only in this limited domain that differences between children and adults might emerge.

CHAPTER 6

The Structure of Universal Asymmetries and Beyond

The last two chapters dealt with two apparently unrelated phenomena, namely children's interpretation of the universal quantifier *every* and their interpretation of the indefinite *some* with respect to negation. Unrelated as those phenomena might appear to be, their investigation has undergone a surprisingly similar development. Taking the case of *every*, children's non-adult behavior was initially interpreted by some researchers as a grammatical phenomenon, but recent research attributes children's non-adult behavior to factors outside the grammar (see Chapter 4 and discussion in Meroni, 2002). As for the interpretation of *some* in negative sentences, Musolino (1998) and Musolino, Crain and Thornton (2000) attributed children's non-adult responses to differences in the grammar of children and adults; this, too, is now more accurately viewed as a non-grammatical phenomenon, observable both in children and adults, and eliminable in children (see Chapter 5). Observations of the course of scientific investigations aside, an interesting relationship between these two phenomena is suggested by recent work on positive polarity items. As we observed in Chapter 1, the standard view of positive polarity items is that these items manifest the opposite pattern of behavior than negative polarity items. Roughly, positive polarity items cannot appear in the scope of downward entailing operators, while negative polarity items must be in the scope of a downward entailing operator. This view has been challenged, however, by Szabolcsi (2002a). Details aside, Szabolcsi argues that one should not focus on so-called positive polarity items (PPIs) in isolation. Rather, one should investigate what properties, if any, are manifested by complex expressions consisting of positive polarity items and the downward entailing operators they 'resist.'

To illustrate the novelty of this account, consider (1).

(1)   *John does not like Mary somewhat.

The standard view focuses on the item *somewhat* and concludes that this item is not compatible with some property of the element *not*, e.g., anti-additivity. By contrast, the research strategy suggested by Szabolcsi is to focus on the complex expression consisting of negation and *somewhat*, considered as a whole. We will refer to this complex item as [*not … somewhat*].

We describe Szabolcsi's proposal in more detail in the next section. To motivate our interest in her proposal, we note here that downward entailment plays an unanticipated role in Szabolcsi's account of the distribution of positive polarity items like *someone* and *somewhat*. We propose to extend Szabolcsi (2002a), to include the relative scope assignment of indefinite noun phrases containing *some* with respect to negation. Importantly, this phenomenon turns out to be sensitive to downward entailment. Thus, Szabolcsi's account provides us with yet another context that can be used to assess children's semantic competence as it pertains to their interpretation of the universal quantifier and their interpretation of the indefinite *some* in negative sentences.

6.1 Positive Polarity as Negative Polarity

The analysis of positive polarity offered by Szabolcsi (2002a) starts from the following contrast, discussed by Baker (1970) and Jespersen (1909-1949).

(2)   John didn't call someone.

(3)   No one thinks that John didn't call someone.

The sentence in (2) can only receive a 'non-isomorphic' interpretation. In other words, the sentence is unacceptable on the interpretation in which *someone* is interpreted in the scope of negation (i.e., (2) does not mean that John did not call anyone). By contrast, (3) can receive an 'isomorphic' interpretation (i.e., (3) can be interpreted as meaning that no one thinks that John didn't call *anyone*).

The generalization offered by Szabolcsi (2002a; p. 13, emphasis in text) is the following:

"PPI do not occur in the immediate scope of a clausemate antiadditive operator AA-Op, unless [AA-OP>PPI] itself is in an NPI-licensing context."

Consider again the contrast between (2) and (3). In (2), the scope assignment in which *someone* receives narrow scope under negation is unacceptable, because negation is antiadditive. [1] The same relative scope assignment becomes acceptable, however, if *someone* is in the scope of the antiadditive operator *not* and, in turn, *not* appears inside the scope of a second downward entailing operator (i.e., an environment that licenses NPIs), such as *No one* in (3). In this way, the analysis by Szabolcsi attempts to specify (a) what features of negation dictate the absence of the isomorphic interpretation for (2) and (b) what features of the determiner *No* are relevant for the availability of the isomorphic interpretation for (3).

The analysis developed by Szabolcsi (2002a) makes reference to the rich typology of polarity items witnessed across natural languages. Concentrating on the polarity item *someone*, Szabolcsi argues that this item is sensitive to the semantic property of antiadditivity. In particular, an item like *someone* 'resists' antiadditivity. Thus, *someone* cannot be interpreted in the scope of negation, which is antiadditive, but it can be interpreted in the scope of a merely downward entailing operator like *at most five* as illustrated by the contrast between (4) and (5).

(4)   John didn't call someone   (*not>someone)

(5)   At most five boys called someone   ($\sqrt{}$at most five boys>someone)

Turning now to the complex consisting of negation and *someone*, Szabolcsi argues that downward entailment is the relevant property for the licensing of the complex item [*not* ... *someone*]. The isomorphic interpretation of this complex expression [*not* ... *someone*] is possible in the scope of a downward entailing - though not necessarily antiadditive – operator, as illustrated in (6). In short, the isomorphic interpretation of the complex item [*not...someone*] is licensed by a downward entailing operator.

---

1 The class of antiadditive operators was introduced in Chapter 1, Section 1.1.3. Recall that antiadditive operators are operators that license inferences in accordance with (both directions) of the first De Morgan's law, i.e., OP_{DE} (A or B) $\Leftrightarrow$ OP_{DE}A and OP_{DE}B.

(6)   At most five boys think that John didn't call someone
                        (at most five boys>not>someone)

To describe these facts one can say that (a) the lexical item *someone* cannot appear in the scope of operators that license negative polarity items like *yet* (i.e., an antiadditive environment) unless (b) the complex item constituted by negation and *someone* appears in the scope of an operator that licenses negative polarity items like *any* or *ever* (i.e., a downward entailing environment).

According to Szabolcsi, the technical implementation of this description makes use of two different features. In particular, items like *someone* are represented as a cluster of two negations and one existential quantifier, i.e. $\neg\neg\exists$. The two negative operators differ, however. One negative operator carries a feature that is sensitive to antiadditivity, while the second negative operator carries a feature that is sensitive to downward entailment. We will use the symbols $\neg_{AA}$ and $\neg_{DE}$ to refer to these operators respectively. In 'ordinary' contexts, the two negative operators do not produce any consequence; both negative features are dormant and the two negative operators cancel each other out. This is what happens in a sentence like (7).

(7)   John called someone
                $\neg_{AA} \ \neg_{DE} \ \exists$

If an antiadditive operator is present, however, that operator activates both features and enters in a resumptive relation with one of the two negation operators, i.e., the antiadditivity-sensitive negation (see De Swart and Sag, 2002).[2] This is illustrated in (8).

(8)   *John didn't call   someone
            OP$_{AA}$ $\neg_{AA} \ \neg_{DE} \ \exists$

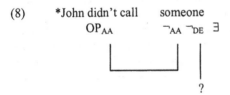

---

2 Roughly, the expression "resumptive quantification" refers to the analysis of multiple occurrences of a monadic quantifier as a single occurrence of a polyadic quantifier (see May, 1989; Ladusaw, 1992).

This, in turn, leaves the negation operator sensitive to downward entailment in search of an operator with which it can enter in a resumptive relation. If no such operator is available, the sentence is unacceptable (on the relevant isomorphic interpretation).

If a second downward entailing operator is present, however, then that operator enters in a resumptive relation with the negative operator sensitive to downward entailment. Thus, the sentence is acceptable (on the relevant isomorphic interpretation).

(9)   At most five boys think that John didn't call   someone

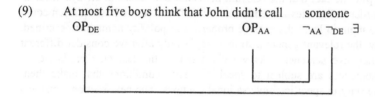

As Szabolcsi acknowledges, one should not focus too much on the details of the proposal. This holds for the particular features that are attributed to the two negations that are part of the representation of *someone*, as well as for the particular mechanisms by which these features interact with other operators. Rather, the focus should be on the enterprise of explaining positive polarity items and negative polarity items using the same features and mechanisms. If we were to ignore Szabolcsi's descriptive generalization, we would be led to describe positive and negative polarity items using different notions, namely the resistance to and the licensing by (potentially different classes of) downward entailing operators. In light of the generalization proposed by Szabolcsi, however, the notion of licensing alone will suffice. The difference between so-called positive and negative polarity items will follow, depending on whether the item to be licensed is a simple polarity item like *any* or a complex item like [*not … someone*].

The account proposed by Szabolcsi (2002a) is interesting for a second reason. Szabolcsi's analysis proposes a change in perspective for linguists to take. The details of the proposal might be wrong. But, the data suggest that the research strategy is right. In particular, we are more likely to gain insight into the properties of items like *someone* if we do not consider them in isolation, but rather as constituents of complex clusters of expressions.

This Copernican move appears to make the child's task all the more difficult, however. First, the child has to learn that an item like *someone* cannot occur in the scope of an antiadditive operator. In addition, the child has to learn to override the resistance to that antiadditive operator if both that operator and the positive polarity item occur within the scope of a downward entailing operator. More generally, the child must take into account some abstract property like antiadditivity when interpreting sentences like *John didn't call someone*. The child must also be able to constrain the role of that abstract property on the basis of another abstract property, namely downward entailment, when interpreting sentences like *No one thinks that John didn't call someone*. To make matters worse, these linguistically motivated distinctions must be drawn despite the fact that the relevant items *not* and *someone* always occur in the same order in the relevant sentences. It is difficult to see how children could rely on the input to learn the evasive properties of polarity items just described. As we saw, the relevant generalization emerges only after we consider different kinds of negative sentences. As we discussed in the last chapter, however, negative sentences are subject to specific felicity conditions that make them appropriate only in specific conversational contexts. The next section considers Szabolcsi's account from the acquisitionist perspective.

6.2 The Universal Asymmetry of the Universal Quantifier Revisited

The phenomena discussed by Szabolcsi (2002a) fit well within the goals of the present study. Regardless of the merit of the specific proposal by Szabolcsi, these phenomena provide us with a generalization in need of an explanation. From the acquisitionist's point of view, the phenomena provide us with additional "specific contingent facts about natural languages" (Pullum and Scholz, 2002; p. 10). One thing that makes the phenomenon interesting is that it points to a generalization at considerable distance from the input. The generalization has to do with a semantic property we have discussed before, namely downward entailment. In turn, this property invites us to consider one more time children's understanding of the universal quantifier *every*, in light of the fact that the two arguments of the universal quantifier *every* differ with respect to downward entailment. Let us review some relevant examples.

(10)　　Every boy who ate cheese pizza or pepperoni pizza got sick
　　　　⇔　　Every boy who ate cheese pizza got sick and every boy who ate pepperoni pizza got sick.

(11)   Every boy ate cheese pizza or pepperoni pizza
                *⇔   Every boy ate cheese pizza and every boy ate
                        pepperoni pizza.

As the following examples indicate, the first argument of *every* licenses the occurrence of the complex negative polarity item [*not ... somewhat*], but the second argument does not.

(12)   Every boy who doesn't like pizza somewhat ordered lasagna.

(13)   *Every boy doesn't like pizza somewhat.

From the point of view of the experimentalist, it is of interest to observe that the two arguments of the universal quantifier *every* also differ when it comes to the interpretation of negation and indefinite noun phrases containing *some*.[3] Consider the sentences in (14) and (15).

(14)   Every boy who didn't eat some pizza is hungry.

(15)   Every boy didn't eat some pizza.

Taking (15) first, we see a familiar pattern. In particular, this sentence can only receive an interpretation in which the indefinite *some* takes scope over negation. Setting aside the question of what scope relationship obtains between *some* and *every*, (16) paraphrases one possible interpretation for (15).[4]

(16)   For every boy, there is some pizza that he didn't eat.

By contrast, the meaning paraphrased in (17) is not a possible interpretation of (15).

(17)   Every boy didn't eat any pizza.

---

3 Specific indefinites were not the major concern of Szabolcsi (2002a), despite being discussed as negative polarity items by Ladusaw (1979; 1980). However, it is useful to bring these items into the picture if one wants to assess the truth-conditional differences between the constructions under consideration. A similar move is adopted by Farkas (2002), who ultimately presents a different solution than Szabolcsi's.
    4 See Beghelli (1995).

This brings us to (14), where the polarity effect on *some* has disappeared; (14) can receive an interpretation according to which the indefinite *some* is in the scope of negation, as in (18).

(18)   Every boy who didn't eat <u>any</u> pizza is hungry.[5]

By contrast, (19) is not a natural interpretation of (14).

(19)   Every boy for whom there is some pizza that he did not eat is hungry.

Thus, the contrast between (14) and (15) mirrors the contrast between (12) and (13). The difference is that the former pertains to the availability of a particular interpretation, while the latter pertains to the grammaticality of the entire sentence. In what follows, we focus on the truth-conditional consequences of these observations, as they can be assessed using a Truth Value Judgment task.

Before we turn to the laboratory, let us comment further on the relevance of this research for our purposes. First, the pattern discussed by Szabolcsi represents a specific contingent fact that adult speakers have mastered during the course of grammar formation. The difficulty of the task is striking, considering that both kinds of sentences we have considered are potentially ambiguous. Focusing on (15), repeated below as (20), we see three scope bearing elements: *every*, *not* and *some*.

(20)   <u>Every</u> boy did<u>n't</u> eat <u>some</u> pizza.

The availability of three scope bearing elements generates six logically possible scope assignments, informally represented below:

(21)   a.   Every>not>some
         b.   Every>some>not
         c.   Some>every>not
         d.   Not>every>some
         e.   Not>some>every
         f.   Some>not>every

---

5 We are mainly concerned with the scope relationship between negation and the indefinite introduced by *some* here. It is still true, however, that a sentence with *some* (e.g., (14)) does not share the information strength associated with the use of *any* (see Kadmon and Landman, 1993).

The question is how children can navigate through this complex quantificational space and ultimately exclude all the interpretations in which *some* occurs in the scope of negation, and in particular (21)a. Furthermore, the child's task is to make sense of three scope bearing elements that occur with the same linear order, but in a different syntactic configuration, as in (14), repeated below as (22).

(22)   Every boy who didn't eat some pizza was hungry.

Of course the linguist might object that the grammatical operations that are needed to interpret (20) are different from the grammatical operations that are needed to interpret (22).[6] After all, two of the scope bearing elements (*not* and *some*) occur in the first argument of the third scope bearing element *every* in (22), whereas they occur in its second argument in (20). Such reasoning, however, refers to 'primitives' that children lack, according to some models of language acquisition (see our discussion of Pullum and Scholz (2002) and Tomasello (2000) in Chapters 1 and 3). Furthermore, this line of reasoning assumes an adult mapping between syntax and semantics. This mapping does not necessarily hold for children, according to some accounts of quantification (see Chapter 4). If one had to choose one phenomenon where children would make wrong generalizations, the contrast between (20) and (22) looks like a good place to start.

6.3 Experimental Design

In this section we illustrate the design and the results of two experiments conducted to investigate children's interpretation of *some* with respect to negation in the two arguments of *every*.

6.3.1 Experiment VI

The first experiment focuses on the first argument of the universal quantifier *every*. In particular, we are interested in determining if the isomorphic

---

6 For extensive discussion of mechanisms that account for scope assignments of indefinites, see Matthewson (1999), Reinhart (1997) and Winter (1997).

interpretation of negation and the indefinite *some* is available to children when those elements appear in that argument. Let us look at one relevant example:

(23)   Every farmer who didn't clean some animal has a broom.

Our interest is whether children can access the isomorphic interpretation paraphrased in (24), and represented more formally as in (25).

(24)   Every farmer who didn't clean any animal has a broom.

(25) $\forall x((\text{farmer}(x) \ \& \ \neg \exists y(\ \text{animal}(y) \ \& \ (x)\text{cleaned}(y))) \rightarrow (x)\text{has a broom})$

In particular, we want to distinguish the interpretation paraphrased in (24) from another logically possible interpretation in which *some* is interpreted outside the scope of negation. This interpretation is paraphrased in (26) and is represented more formally in (27).

(26)   Every farmer such that there is an animal that he did not clean has a broom.

(27) $\forall x(\text{farmer}(x) \ \& \ \exists y(\ \text{animal}(y) \ \& \ \neg(x)\text{cleaned}(y))) \rightarrow (x)\text{has a broom})$

Let us now turn to the context that would distinguish between (24) and (26) as possible interpretations of (23). The two interpretations differ in the farmers that are required to have a broom. Two sets can be considered: the set of farmers who did not clean any animals and the set of farmers who did not clean some of the animals they were supposed to clean. Now, one can also describe the farmers who did not clean any animals as farmers for whom one can find some animals that they did not clean. Thus, the set of farmers who did not clean any animals is a subset of the set of farmers for which there are animals that they did not clean. As a consequence, to distinguish between the isomorphic interpretation in (24) and the non-isomorphic interpretation in (26), one can only consider a context in which the isomorphic interpretation is true and the non-isomorphic interpretation in (26) is false. Let us now illustrate how this was achieved, by considering a typical trial.

(28)   "This is a story about five farmers and their boss, the Indian. The Indian says: "Guys, it is time to get to work. I think you should start by cleaning the animals, because they are very dirty" and he points to five pigs, five horses and five chicks. Then, he adds: "I think each one of

you has to clean three animals: one pig, one horse and one chick." The first farmer says: "Ok, I think he is right, these animals are very dirty" and he cleans the pig, the horse and the chick that the Indian has brought in front of him." The second farmer says: "Ok, it is my turn now" and he cleans the horse and the chick. Then, he looks at the pig that the Indian has brought in front of him and says: "Why should I clean the pig? I bet it is gonna get all muddy anyway. I am sorry Indian, but I do not want to clean the pig." The remaining three farmers look at the animals that the Indian has brought in front of them and start complaining about how useless it is to clean the animals and then one of them says: "I am sorry, but we are tired of this. We clean the animals, and as soon as we are finished they get dirty again. We don't wanna do this!" Then, the Indian reappears holding five brooms and says: "Well, let me see if you did what I asked you to do. The Indian sees that the first farmer cleaned what he asked him to. When the Indian gets to the second farmer, he says: "Well, you cleaned the horse and the chick but you did not clean the pig. You have been a bit lazy. Maybe I'll find something else for you to do!" Then he gets to the last three farmers and says "I am very disappointed, the animals are so dirty! Why didn't you guys clean them? I think this is not fair. Since you did not want to clean the animals, you should at least clean the barn" and he gives a broom to each one of the three farmers. Then, the Indian considers giving a broom to the farmer who did not clean the pig but decides against it."

At this point, the puppet, who was manipulated by the second experimenter offered the target sentence preceded by the (positive) linguistic antecedent as in (29).[7]

(29)   This was a story about five farmers and one Indian. Every farmer had to clean three animals and I know what happened. <u>Every farmer who didn't clean some animal has a broom.</u>

---

7 The role of positive lead-ins for the interpretation of negative sentences was discussed in Chapter 5. For the present purposes, it is irrelevant whether the target sentence is felicitous because a positive lead-in is available or because the positive lead-in that is available explicitly mentions the expected outcome.

Notice that the context makes the target sentence true if negation and *some* are interpreted in the order in which they occur (see (30)). In fact, the three farmers who did not clean any animal received a broom.

(30)   Every farmer who did<u>n't</u> clean <u>any</u> animal has a broom.

By contrast, the context makes the sentence false on the non-isomorphic reading paraphrased in (31).

(31)   Every farmer for whom there is <u>some</u> animal that he did<u>n't</u> clean has a broom.

To see why the target sentence in (30) is false on the interpretation paraphrased in (31), we need to consider that there are four farmers for whom one can find some animal that they did not clean: the three farmers who did not clean any animal as well as the farmer who did not clean the pig. However not every farmer in this group received a broom. Thus the sentence is false on the non-isomorphic interpretation under consideration.

According to our reading of Szabolcsi's proposal, the isomorphic interpretation of the complex item [*not...some*] is licensed in the first argument of *every*, a downward entailing environment. Thus, the experimental hypothesis was that children and adults would consistently accept the target sentences. In the case at hand, the affirmative response was expected on the grounds that the farmers who had not cleaned any animal had indeed received a broom.

Fifteen children participated in a Truth Value Judgment task. Children ranged in age from 3;10 to 5;08, with mean age of 4;08. Each child was presented with four target trials. Those trials were preceded by one warm-up trial and they were interspersed with filler trials to balance the number of 'yes' and 'no' responses. Let us turn to the results. Children accepted the target sentence 53 times out of 60 trials (88%). Importantly, when children were asked to motivate their (affirmative) responses by pointing to "what made Kermit right," they consistently pointed to the farmers who had not cleaned any animal. A group of 24 undergraduates participated as adult controls in a videotaped version of the experiment. They accepted the target sentences 87 times out of 94 trials (92.5%).[8]

---

8 Two adult subjects did not respond to one of the target trials.

Thus, children consistently access the isomorphic interpretation of the complex item *[not ... some N]*, when this item occurs in the first argument of the universal quantifier *every*, a downward entailing environment.

6.3.2 Experiment VII

The next experiment focuses on the second argument of the universal quantifier *every*. In particular, we are interested in determining if children can interpret negation and *some* in a non-isomorphic way, when those elements occur in the second argument of the universal quantifier. A relevant sentence is reported below.

(32)   <u>Every</u> farmer did<u>n't</u> clean <u>some</u> animal.

As in Experiment VI, our interest is in the relative scope assignment of negation and *some*. The findings from Experiment VI show that children access the isomorphic interpretation of these operators when they occur in the first argument of the universal quantifier *every*. The question is whether or not children access the same scope assignment when negation and *some* occur in the second argument of *every*. In the case of (32), the question is whether children's interpretation is limited to the isomorphic interpretation paraphrased in (33) and represented in (34).

(33)   Every farmer didn't clean any animal.

(34) $\forall x(\text{farmer}(x) \rightarrow \neg \exists y(\text{animal}(y) \,\&\, (x)\text{cleaned}(y)))$

In particular, we want to distinguish the interpretation paraphrased in (33) from another interpretation, in which *some* is interpreted outside the scope of negation as in the paraphrase in (35) and the representation in (36).[9]

(35)   For every farmer, there is an animal that he did not clean.

---

9 (36) is *one* possible non-isomorphic scope assignment for (32). In our discussion, we will not consider the relative scope of *some* and *every* and we will only consider the relative scope of negation and *some*. For discussion of the possible scope assignments for (32) we refer the reader to Beghelli (1995).

(36) $\forall x(\text{farmer}(x) \rightarrow \exists y(\text{animal}(y) \ \& \ \neg(x)\text{cleaned}(y)))$

Let us now consider what context would distinguish between the interpretations paraphrased in (33) and (35).[10] If every farmer did not clean any animals, then there are also some animals that the farmers did not clean. The converse is not true, however. Thus, to distinguish between the isomorphic interpretation in (33) and the non-isomorphic interpretation in (35), one has to consider a context in which the isomorphic interpretation is false and the non-isomorphic interpretation under consideration is true. Let us now illustrate how this was achieved, by considering a typical trial.

(37)   "This is a story about three farmers and their boss, the Indian. The Indian says: "Guys, it is time to get to work. I think you should start by cleaning the animals, because they are very dirty" and he points to three pigs, three horses and three chicks. Then, he adds: "I think each one of you has to clean three animals: one pig, one horse and one chick." The farmers get to work, and each farmer cleans the particular horse that the Indian brought in front of him. Then, one of the farmers says: "Ok, I think we are done now!" The Indian says: "I don't think so! Now, you must clean the pigs and the chicks." The farmers get to work again. Each farmer cleans the chick that the Indian brought in front of him and then one of farmers says: "Ok, now we are done!" The Indian protests and reminds them that they are supposed to clean all the animals. The farmers consider cleaning the pigs, but conclude that it would be useless."

At this point, the puppet manipulated by the second experimenter offered the target sentence preceded by the (positive) linguistic antecedent as in (38).

(38)   This was a story about three farmers and one Indian. Every farmer had to clean three animals and I know what happened. <u>Every farmer didn't clean some animal.</u>

Notice that the context makes the target sentence false if negation and *some* are interpreted in the order in which they occur (see (39)).

---

10 In this particular case, the relevant context is constructed along the same lines discussed by Musolino (1998), as described in Chapter 5.

(39)   Every farmer did<u>n't</u> clean <u>any</u> animal.

In fact, all three farmers cleaned some animal. This makes it false that they did not clean any animal. By contrast, the context makes the sentence (felicitous and) true on the non-isomorphic reading, which is paraphrased in (40).

(40)   For <u>every</u> farmer, there is <u>some</u> animal that he did<u>n't</u> clean.

In particular, on the interpretation paraphrased in (40) the target sentence in (38) is true because, for every farmer, there are is some animal that farmer did not clean, namely the pigs.[11]
    Let us now consider the predictions of our reading of Szabolcsi's account. According to the account introduced in Section 6.1, the antiadditivity of negation prevents the indefinite *some* from receiving narrow scope under negation. Furthermore, in (38) the isomorphic interpretation of the complex item [*not...some*] is not rescued by the universal quantifier *every*, because negation and *some* occur in its second argument, a non-downward entailing environment. Thus, the experimental hypothesis was that children and adults would consistently access the non-isomorphic interpretation of the target sentence. In the case at hand, the non-isomorphic interpretation makes the sentence true: there is indeed some animal that every farmer didn't clean, namely the pig that each farmer was supposed to clean.
    Fifteen children participated in a Truth Value Judgment task. Children ranged in age from 4;01 to 5;05, with a mean age of 4;09. Each child was presented with four target trials. The target trials were preceded by one warm-up trial and they were interspersed with filler trials to balance the number of 'yes' and 'no' responses. Turning to the results, children accepted the target sentence 47 times out of 60 trials (78%). A group of 17 undergraduates participated in a videotaped version of the experiment as adult controls. They correctly accepted the target sentences 57 times out of 68 trials (82.4%).
    To sum up, children consistently accessed a non-isomorphic interpretation of the complex item [*not ... some N*], when this item occurred in the second argument of the universal quantifier *every*, an upward entailing environment.

---

11 Again, despite the choice of a particular paraphrase that makes the sentence true, the context does not allow us to distinguish the relative scope of the universal and the existential quantifier. All we can conclude is that the context distinguishes between the isomorphic vs. non-isomorphic interpretation of the two scope bearing elements *not* and *some*.

6.3.3 Summary of the Experimental Findings

Before we discuss the relevance of the findings, it is worth discussing a possible objection to the experimental design. As the reader may have noticed, the experimental hypothesis was associated with the affirmative answer in both Experiment VI and VII. This was not a matter of choice, however. As we discussed in Chapter 5, in 'ordinary' contexts the interpretation in which *some* receives narrow scope under negation entails the interpretation in which *some* receives wider scope than negation. Thus, one can only seek to determine if the latter interpretation is available. Now, in the first argument of *every*, the opposite is true. Thus, one can only seek to determine if the isomorphic interpretation is available.

In addition to being the only logical option, the experimental design can be defended on further grounds. The main reason why the response associated with the experimental hypothesis should be a negative answer is that children usually respond affirmatively if they are confused about the experiment (see Grimshaw and Rosen, 1990). In the particular case at hand, however, the findings of previous research on the structures under consideration have not conformed to this assumption. Recall the original finding on children's interpretation of the universal quantifier *every*. In the Inhelder and Piaget study, children were reported to unexpectedly *reject* the target sentences containing the universal quantifier. The same holds for the original study on children's interpretation of negative sentences containing negation and the indefinite *some*. As we discussed in Chapter 5, Musolino (1998) found that children as old as 5;9 unexpectedly *rejected* the target sentences. Importantly, the same behavior emerged in one of the conditions of Experiment V, reported in Chapter 5.[12]

---

12 Still, a reasonable question to ask is whether children ever say 'no' to sentences containing three scope bearing elements. To address this question a study employing the Truth Value Judgment task is currently being conducted. In the study, children are presented with stories similar to the ones illustrated for Experiment VI and VII. The stories are slightly different, however, so that the target sentences do not correctly describe the final outcome of the story. To illustrate, the story about the five farmers described in (28) would be modified so that in the end only two of the farmers who did not clean any animals would receive a broom, while the third farmer who did not clean any animal would receive a shovel. Similarly, the story about three farmers described in (37), would be modified so that one of the farmers would eventually clean all the animals

Finally, to ensure that children accepted the target sentences for the right reason, children were occasionally asked to motivate their answer by pointing to the characters "that made Kermit right." Children consistently pointed to the appropriate objects. For example, when children accepted the sentence *Every farmer didn't clean some animal* relatively to the context described in (37), they correctly pointed to the pigs as the animals that made Kermit right. Similarly, when children accepted the sentence *Every farmer who didn't clean some animal has a broom* relatively to the context described in (28), they correctly pointed to the three farmers who had not cleaned any animal.

It must be said that the relevance of the experimental results cannot be fully understood until one can determine whether the relevant sentences are actually unambiguous for (at least some of the) children. The results from Experiment V reported in Chapter 5 show that half of the children would always interpret the indefinite *some* outside the scope of negation. Unfortunately, the fact that the non-isomorphic interpretation corresponded to an affirmative answer makes our interpretation of the experimental findings tentative. Further research should attempt to determine whether an effect of downward entailingness for the resolution of scope ambiguities can also be observed in cases in which the experimental hypothesis is not associated with a 'yes' answer (e.g., with sentences containing the numeral *two*).

With these considerations in mind, the findings of Experiment VI and VII are compatible with the hypothesis that children's resolution of scope ambiguity between *not* and *some* is sensitive to some abstract property of the environment in which these operators occur. In particular, children (like adults) assign narrow scope to *some* if negation and *some* occur in a downward entailing environment, but they assign wide scope to *some* if the two operators occur in a non-downward entailing environment.

The particular pair of environments that we considered makes the results relevant in yet another respect. In Chapter 4 we illustrated how children's interpretation of sentences containing the universal quantifier *every* has led to the hypothesis that children fail to distinguish between the first and the second argument of the universal quantifier. In that chapter, we also presented some experimental evidence suggesting that this hypothesis is unwarranted. In particular, the experimental evidence suggests that children know that the

---

that the Indian brought in front of him. The preliminary results from a group of 10 children show that, when the stories were modified in the way described above, four and five year olds reject target sentences like *Every farmer who didn't clean some animal has a broom* and *Every farmer didn't clean some animal* over 80% of the time.

disjunction operator *or* is interpreted differently in the two arguments of the universal quantifier *every*. The results documented in the present chapter extend the evidence showing children's knowledge of the semantics of the universal quantifier *every*. In particular, the relative scope assignment of *some* and *not* was used as a criterion for upward entailingness. Importantly, the results of Experiment VII suggest that children know that the second argument of the universal quantifier does not constitute a downward entailing environment and are not obscured by the factors that surfaced in the Boster and Crain study or in our own Experiment IV. Children's knowledge of the difference between the two arguments of the universal quantifier *every* surfaces in another domain, as predicted by linguistic theory.

6.4 Conclusion

This chapter presented a preliminary study on children's knowledge of the interaction between positive polarity and negative polarity. Our discussion drew upon a proposal by Szabolcsi (2002a), who argued that there is a correlation between the abstract linguistic property of downward entailment and the relative scope assignment of items like negation and *some*. From a logical point of view, there is no reason why this correlation should hold. One can imagine a language in which the entailment properties of a linguistic environment do not play any role in how negation and *some* are interpreted. This is not the case of English, however. Thus, for a child to be able to learn any possible language, the child has to be able to draw the distinction that holds in English. In other words, the child has to be able to consider the possibility that the relative scope of items like negation and *some* is influenced by some abstract property of the environment in which those elements occur. By contrast, no child should be limited to the hypothesis that the relative scope of items like negation and *some* is influenced by less abstract, but more visible, features such as the simple occurrence of a third scope bearing element.

In Chapter 1, we highlighted several quirks of the way natural languages make use of entailment relations. First, we observed that some positive polarity items can occur in downward entailing environments, as long as some operation of the grammar allows these items to be interpreted outside the scope of the relevant downward entailing operator. Second, we have illustrated how this grammatical operation does not need to take place if two negative operators are present. Again, there is no reason why natural languages should instantiate either of these properties. It is logically possible that children approach the language acquisition process without assuming the existence of covert grammatical operations. Moreover, it is logically possible that children approach the task of language acquisition assuming that the interpretation of items like negation and *some* is determined once and for all, in virtue of the linguistic environment they appear in most frequently, for example. Although logically possible, the experimental findings suggest that both these scenarios are implausible. We have repeatedly highlighted what we take to be the main thrust of Szabolcsi's proposal, a change in perspective that only makes sense from the point of view of linguistic theory. Despite its promissory character, linguists have failed to adopt this change in perspective for a long time. Apparently, children never had any doubt about it.

The experimental results presented in this final chapter represent the first steps of a novel research program. Although a number of issues remain to be addressed, the research introduced here is the natural outcome of the picture emerging from this dissertation.

We began our investigation of polarity phenomena in child language by considering three different models of language acquisition. As we progressed towards more and more complicated phenomena, we observed that the Conservative Learning model and the Rich Input model could not even begin to account for children's behavior. By contrast, we have encountered no evidence against the Continuity Assumption as yet, even when occasional mismatches between children's and adults' behavior have surfaced. The next step is to accept Continuity Assumption as the null assumption for child language research. Even in the domain of semantic competence, there is no reason to assume that child language differs from adult language in ways that would exceed the boundary conditions imposed by Universal Grammar.

Experimental Materials

Experiment I

Experimental Stimuli

Trial 1

Characters and Story: Three monkeys are looking for three pieces of grapefruit, a banana and a Frisbee that a Rabbit hid. Initially, each monkey finds some grapefruit and then one also finds the banana.

Target Sentence for children in Group I: None of the monkeys found the banana or the Frisbee.
Target Sentence for children in Group II: Every monkey found some grapefruit, but none of the monkeys found the banana or the Frisbee.

Trial 2
See Chapter 2

Trial 3
Characters and Story: Three dogs, one penguin and one panda bear ask three dolphins if they can ride them. The dolphins initially give a ride to the dogs. Then, one dolphin also agrees on giving a ride to the penguin.

<u>Target Sentence for children in Group I</u>: None of the dolphins carried the penguin or the panda bear.
<u>Target Sentence for children in Group II</u>: Every dolphin carried a dog, but none of the dolphins carried the penguin or the panda bear.

Trial 4
<u>Characters and Story</u>: Three polar bears want to play with Donald Duck's toys. Donald Duck has three skateboards, a Frisbee and a basketball. The polar bears initially choose the skate-boards, but then one also takes the basketball.

<u>Target Sentence for children in Group I</u>: None of the polar bears chose the Frisbee or the basketball.
<u>Target Sentence for children in Group II</u>: Every polar bear chose a skateboard, but none of the polar bears chose the Frisbee or the basketball.

Individual Subject Results

Individual results from children in Group I

	Age	Trial 1	Trial 2	Trial 3	Trial 4
Child 1	3;10;26	NO	NO	NO	NO
Child 2	4;00;14	NO	YES	YES	YES
Child 3	4;01;05	NO	NO	YES	NO
Child 4	4;01;08	NO	NO	NO	NO
Child 5	4;02;20	NO	NO	YES	NO
Child 6	4;03;25	NO	YES	NO	NO
Child 7	4;04;07	NO	NO	YES	NO
Child 8	4;04;18	NO	NO	NO	NO
Child 9	4;05;17	YES	YES	YES	YES
Child 10	4;06;04	NO	NO	NO	NO
Child 11	4;06;07	NO	NO	NO	NO
Child 12	5;05;03	NO	NO	NO	NO
Child 13	5;07;25	NO	NO	NO	NO
Child 14	5;08;04	NO	NO	NO	NO
Child 15	5;10;05	NO	NO	NO	YES

Individual results from children in Group II

	Age	Trial 1	Trial 2	Trial 3	Trial 4
Child 1	4;01;28	YES	NO	NO	NO
Child 2	4;02;01	NO	NO	NO	NO
Child 3	4;02;22	NO	NO	NO	NO
Child 4	4;02;27	NO	NO	NO	NO
Child 5	4;04;05	NO	NO	NO	NO
Child 6	4;04;17	NO	NO	NO	NO
Child 7	4;05;05	NO	NO	NO	NO
Child 8	4;06;09	NO	NO	NO	NO
Child 9	4;07;07	YES	NO	NO	NO
Child 10	4;08;01	NO	NO	NO	NO
Child 11	4;08;09	NO	NO	NO	NO
Child 12	4;08;18	NO	NO	NO	NO
Child 13	4;10;25	NO	NO	NO	NO
Child 14	5;00;12	YES	NO	NO	NO
Child 15	5;08;18	NO	NO	NO	NO

Experiment II

Experimental Stimuli

Trial 1
See Chapter 3

Trial 2
Characters and Story: Snow-white takes Grumpy to Genie's store. Genie has a lot of food (a strawberry, a hot-dog and bottle of mustard) but he tells Snow-white that the mustard and the strawberry fell in the magic potion. After the puppet's prediction, Snow-white decides that grumpy can have the strawberry.

Target Sentence: I predict that Snow-white will not let Grumpy eat the magic mustard or the magic strawberry.

Individual Subject Results

	Age	Trial 1	Trial 2
Child 1	3;08;06	YES	YES
Child 2	3;08;20	NO	NO
Child 3	3;10;02	NO	NO
Child 4	3;10;13	NO	NO
Child 5	3;10;14	NO	NO
Child 6	4;01;20	NO	NO
Child 7	4;01;28	NO	NO
Child 8	4;02;04	YES	YES
Child 9	4;03;18	YES	NO
Child 10	4;03;18	NO	NO
Child 11	4;05;12	NO	NO
Child 12	4;05;19	NO	YES
Child 13	4;06;26	NO	YES
Child 14	4;07;17	NO	NO
Child 15	4;08;07	NO	NO
Child 16	4;08;18	NO	YES
Child 17	4;09;13	NO	NO
Child 18	4;05;06	NO	NO
Child 19	4;10;00	NO	NO
Child 20	4;10;07	NO	NO
Child 21	4;11;09	NO	NO
Child 22	5;01;05	NO	NO
Child 23	5;01;26	NO	NO
Child 24	5;03;01	NO	YES
Child 25	5;03;15	NO	NO
Child 26	5;03;26	NO	NO
Child 27	5;05;21	NO	NO
Child 28	5;06;21	NO	NO
Child 29	5;11;03	NO	NO
Child 30	6;05;09	NO	NO

Experiment III

Experimental Stimuli

Trial 1
See Chapter 3

Trial 2
Characters and Story: Tigger made a bet with two trolls that he can jump over them. He jumps over one, but he fails to jump over the second troll so he has to give him some of his things. He has a brush, a skate-board, and a basketball. In the end he gives him the hairbrush.

Target Sentence: Tigger will give the troll he can't jump over the hairbrush or the skateboard.

Individual Subject Results

	Age	Trial 1	Trial 2
Child 1	3;05;03	YES	YES
Child 2	3;08;00	YES	YES
Child 3	3;09;16	NO	NO
Child 4	3;10;26	YES	NO
Child 5	4;01;08	YES	YES
Child 6	4;01;23	NO	NO
Child 7	4;03;09	YES	YES
Child 8	4;04;20	YES	YES
Child 9	4;05;15	YES	YES
Child 10	4;05;27	YES	YES
Child 11	4;06;26	YES	YES
Child 12	4;07;16	YES	YES
Child 13	4;08;05	NO	YES
Child 14	4;08;15	NO	NO
Child 15	4:08;16	YES	YES
Child 16	4;09;11	YES	YES
Child 17	4;09;19	YES	YES
Child 18	4;09;27	YES	NO
Child 19	4;10;06	YES	YES
Child 20	5;00;12	NO	NO
Child 21	5;01;00	YES	YES
Child 22	5;02;21	YES	YES
Child 23	5;02;24	YES	YES
Child 24	5;03;25	YES	YES
Child 25	5;05;08	NO	NO
Child 26	5;05;10	YES	YES
Child 27	5;05;26	YES	YES
Child 28	5;06;24	YES	YES
Child 29	5;07;27	YES	YES
Child 30	5;09;21	YES	YES
Child 31	6;03;29	NO	YES
Child 32	6;03;29	YES	YES
Child 33	6;04;12	YES	YES
Child 34	6;04;25	YES	YES
Child 35	6;05;21	YES	YES

Experiment IV

Experimental Stimuli

Trial 1
See Chapter 4

Trial 2
Characters and Story: Three boys want to get into farming school. The farmer wants to see who could become a good farmer and puts a bunch of objects in front of them: three brooms (two small and one big), three hats (two regular hats and one big hat like the one the farmer is wearing), a chair and a drum. Then he asks the boys to choose the objects that would be helpful to a farmer. One boy takes a small broom, one boy takes a small broom and a regular hat and the last boy only takes a regular hat.

Target Sentence: Every boy chose a broom or a hat.

Trial 3
Characters and Story: Snow-white and three dwarves go on a picnic. Snow-white brings a lot of good food: three bananas (two small and one big), three strawberries (two ripe and one still green), a carrot and a chocolate chip cookie. Snow-white encourages the dwarves to choose something healthy. One dwarf chooses a ripe strawberry, the second dwarf chooses a ripe strawberry and a small banana and the third dwarf chooses a small banana.

Target Sentence: Every dwarf ate a strawberry or a banana.

Trial 4
Characters and Story: Three kiwi birds visit Jar Jar Binks. Jar Jar Binks is very excited and wants to be a good host, so he offers his toys to the kiwi birds. He has three blocks (two small and one big), three skate-boards (two small and one big), a basketball and a tree. The kiwi birds consider all these toys, then one kiwi bird takes a small block, one takes a small block and a small skateboard and the last bird takes a small skate-board.

Target Sentence: Every kiwi bird took a block or a skateboard.

Individual Subject Results

	Age	Trial 1	Trial 2	Trial 3	Trial 4
Child 1	3;10;17	NO	NO	NO	NO
Child 2	3;10;28	YES	NO	NO	NO
Child 3	3;11;28	YES	YES	YES	YES
Child 4	4;03;03	YES	YES	YES	YES
Child 5	4;04;08	YES	YES	YES	YES
Child 6	4;04;19	NO	YES	NO	NO
Child 7	4;05;13	YES	NO	NO	YES
Child 8	4;05;14	NO	NO	NO	NO
Child 9	4;06;06	YES	YES	YES	YES
Child 10	4;06;24	YES	YES	YES	YES
Child 11	4;06;26	YES	NO	NO	YES
Child 12	4;07;11	NO	YES	YES	YES
Child 13	4;07;27	YES	YES	YES	YES
Child 14	4;08;04	YES	YES	YES	YES
Child 15	4;08;25	YES	NO	NO	NO
Child 16	4;10;20	YES	YES	YES	YES
Child 17	4;11;24	YES	NO	YES	YES
Child 18	5;00;12	YES	YES	YES	YES
Child 19	5;02;09	YES	YES	YES	YES
Child 20	5;02;21	YES	YES	YES	YES
Child 21	5;04;09	NO	YES	YES	YES
Child 22	5;08;01	YES	YES	YES	YES
Child 23	5;09;20	YES	NO	NO	NO

Experiment V

Experimental Stimuli

Trial 1
See Chapter 5

Trial 2
Characters and Story: Chuckie is interviewing for a job as a waiter at the restaurant owned by Papa Smurf. Papa Smurf asks Chuckie to put four bottles on the table. Chuckie manages to put two bottles on the table, but drops the remaining two bottles.

Target Sentence for children in Group I: Chuckie didn't put some bottles on the table.
Target Sentence for children in Group II: Chuckie didn't drop some bottles on the floor.

Trial 3
Characters and Story: Grover calls the Troll at the pizza store and asks for four big pizzas. He promises the Troll a big tip if he manages to deliver the pizzas fast. On the way to Grover's house, the Troll starts driving too fast and accidentally drops two pizzas so he arrives at Grover's house with only two pizzas.

Target Sentence for children in Group I: The Troll didn't deliver some pizzas.
Target Sentence for children in Group II: The Troll didn't lose some pizzas.

Trial 4
Characters and Story: Supergirl asks Bart Simpson to safeguard four jewels while she goes shopping. Bart Simpson trips over a log and loses the jewels. He tries to find them, but he can only recover two of the jewels.

Target Sentence for children in Group I: Bart Simpson didn't find some jewels.
Target Sentence for children in Group II: Bart Simpson didn't lose some jewels.

Individual Subject Results

Individual results from children in Group I

	Age	*Trial 1*	*Trial 2*	*Trial 3*	*Trial 4*
Child 1	4;00;20	YES	YES	YES	YES
Child 2	4;01;15	YES	YES	YES	YES
Child 3	4;07;11	YES	YES	YES	YES
Child 4	4;07;29	YES	YES	YES	YES
Child 5	4;08;01	YES	NO	YES	NO
Child 6	4;08;04	NO	YES	YES	YES
Child 7	4;08;07	YES	YES	YES	YES
Child 8	4;08;16	YES	YES	YES	YES
Child 9	4;09;00	YES	YES	YES	YES
Child 10	4;10;26	YES	YES	YES	YES
Child 11	5;00;06	YES	YES	YES	YES
Child 12	5;03;12	YES	YES	YES	YES
Child 13	5;03;17	YES	NO	NO	YES
Child 14	5;04;26	YES	YES	YES	YES
Child 15	5;05;18	YES	NO	YES	YES

Individual results from children in Group II

	Age	*Trial 1*	*Trial 2*	*Trial 3*	*Trial 4*
Child 1	4;01;27	YES	YES	YES	YES
Child 2	4;03;29	NO	YES	YES	YES
Child 3	4;05;20	YES	YES	YES	YES
Child 4	4;06;08	YES	YES	YES	YES
Child 5	4;07;16	NO	YES	YES	NO
Child 6	4;08;16	NO	NO	NO	YES
Child 7	4;11;22	YES	YES	NO	NO
Child 8	5;00;23	NO	NO	YES	YES
Child 9	5;01;10	YES	YES	YES	YES
Child 10	5;01;22	YES	YES	YES	YES
Child 11	5;03;06	NO	NO	NO	NO
Child 12	5;04;18	NO	NO	NO	NO
Child 13	5;05;12	NO	NO	NO	NO
Child 14	5;04;16	NO	NO	NO	NO
Child 15	5;07;18	NO	NO	NO	NO

Experiment VI

Experimental Stimuli

Trial 1
Characters and Story: Peter Pan is going on vacation and he asks his five friends to help him with his animals. He asks each kid to take care of one dog, one dinosaur and one pig. The first kid takes all three animals. The second kid takes the dog and the dinosaur but not the pig. The remaining three kids do not take any animal. Then Peter Pan gives a bucket of paint to each of these three kids, so that they can paint the fence while he is gone. He has a fourth bucket of paint which he keeps.

Target Sentence: Every kid who didn't take care of some animal got some paint.

Trial 2
Characters and Story: The Count is training five dwarves for a jumping competition. He wants every dwarf to jump over a block, a barrel and a chair. The first dwarf jumps over all the three obstacles. The second dwarf jumps over the block and the barrel but decides not to jump over the chair. The remaining three dwarves decide not to jump at all. The Count gives a skate-board to each of these three dwarves, so they can get back in shape. The count has two more skate-boards which he keeps.

Target Sentence: Every dwarf who didn't jump over some obstacle received a skate-board.

Trial 3
See Chapter 6

Trial 4
Characters and Story: Minnie Mouse and five smurves go on a picnic. For each smurf, Minnie Mouse has brought a slice of pizza, a potato chip and some lettuce. One smurf takes the slice of pizza, the potato chip and the lettuce. The second smurf takes the slice of pizza and the potato chip but no lettuce. The remaining three smurves do not take anything. Minnie Mouse tells them that

they have to eat something and gives them a banana. She keeps two other bananas for herself.

<u>Target Sentence</u>: Every smurf who didn't eat some food got a banana.

Individual Subject Results

	Age	Trial 1	Trial 2	Trial 3	Trial 4
Child 1	3;10;01	NO	YES	NO	YES
Child 2	3;10;05	YES	YES	YES	YES
Child 3	4;03;16	YES	YES	NO	YES
Child 4	4;03;29	YES	YES	YES	YES
Child 5	4;05;10	YES	YES	YES	YES
Child 6	4;07;08	YES	YES	YES	YES
Child 7	4;07;27	YES	YES	YES	YES
Child 8	4;08;01	YES	YES	YES	YES
Child 9	4;08;21	YES	YES	YES	YES
Child 10	4;09;24	YES	YES	YES	YES
Child 11	5;01;00	NO	NO	NO	NO
Child 12	5;03;03	YES	YES	YES	YES
Child 13	5;03;10	YES	YES	YES	YES
Child 14	5;05;12	YES	YES	YES	YES
Child 15	5;08;21	YES	YES	YES	YES

Experiment VII

Experimental Stimuli

Trial 1
Characters and Story: Peter Pan is going on vacation and he asks his three friends to help him with his animals. He asks each kid to take care of one dog, one dinosaur and one pig. Each kid takes the dog and the dinosaur, but not the pig.

Target Sentence: Every kid didn't take care of some animal.

Trial 2
Characters and Story: The Count is training three dwarves for a jumping competition. He wants every dwarf to jump over a block, a barrel and a chair. Every dwarf jumps over the block and the barrel, but refuses to jump over the chair.

Target Sentence: Every dwarf didn't jump over some obstacle.

Trial 3
See Chapter 6

Trial 4
Characters and Story: Minnie Mouse and three smurves go on a picnic. For each smurf, Minnie Mouse has brought a slice of pizza, a potato chip and some lettuce. Every smurf takes the slice of pizza and the potato chip, but not the lettuce.

Target Sentence: Every smurf didn't eat some food.

Individual Subject Results

	Age	Trial 1	Trial 2	Trial 3	Trial 4
Child 1	4;01;14	YES	YES	YES	YES
Child 2	4;02;04	NO	NO	YES	YES
Child 3	4;02;24	YES	YES	YES	YES
Child 4	4;05;05	NO	NO	YES	YES
Child 5	4;05;13	NO	NO	NO	NO
Child 6	4;05;25	NO	YES	YES	YES
Child 7	4;06;03	YES	YES	YES	NO
Child 8	4;07;21	YES	YES	YES	YES
Child 9	4;08;27	YES	YES	YES	YES
Child 10	4;10;00	YES	YES	YES	YES
Child 11	5;03;12	YES	YES	YES	YES
Child 12	5;05;07	YES	NO	NO	NO
Child 13	5;05;11	YES	YES	YES	YES
Child 14	5;05;22	YES	YES	YES	YES
Child 15	5;06;11	YES	YES	YES	YES

References

Amidon, Arlene and Peter Carey. 1972. "Why five-year-olds cannot understand "before" and "after"," *Journal of Verbal Learning and Verbal Behavior*, 11, 417-423.

Baker, Carl LeRoy. 1970. "Double negatives," *Linguistic Inquiry*, 1, 169-186.

Barwise, John, and Robin Cooper. 1981. "Generalized quantifiers and natural language," *Linguistics and Philosophy*, 4, 159-219.

Beghelli, Filippo. 1995. *The Phrase Structure of Quantifier Scope*. Ph.D. Dissertation, University of California at Los Angeles.

Bloom, Paul. 2000. *How Children Learn the Meanings of Words*. Cambridge, MA: The MIT Press.

Boster, Carole, and Stephen Crain. 1993. "On Children's Understanding of *Every* and *Or*." In *Proceedings of Early Cognition and Transition to Language*, University of Texas at Austin.

Bucci, Wilma. 1978. "The interpretation of universal affirmative propositions," *Cognition*, 6, 55-57.

Carden, Guy. 1973. *English Quantifiers: Logical Structure and Linguistic Variation*. Tokyo: The Taishukan Publishing Company.

Carey, Susan, and Fei Xu. 1999. "Sortals and Kinds: An Appreciation of John MacNamara." In Ray Jackendoff, Paul Bloom and Karen Wynn (Eds.) *Language, Logic and* Concepts, 311-336. Cambridge, MA: The MIT Press.

Chierchia, Gennaro and Sally McConnell-Ginet. 1990. *Meaning and Grammar*. Cambridge, MA: The MIT Press.

Chierchia, Gennaro. 2002. *Scalar Implicatures, Polarity Phenomena, and the Syntax/Pragmatics Interface*. Ms., Universita' di Milano Bicocca.

Chierchia, Gennaro, Stephen Crain, Maria Teresa Guasti and Rosalind Thornton. 1998. "*Some* and *or*: A study on the Emergence of Logical

Form," in *Proceedings of the Boston University Conference on Language Development*, 22, 97-108. Somerville, MA: Cascadilla Press.

Chomsky, Carol. 1969. *The Acquisition of Syntax in Children from 5 to 10.* Cambridge, MA: The MIT Press.

Chomsky, Noam. 1971. *Problems of knowledge and freedom.* New York, Pantheon.

Chomsky, Noam. 1980a. *Rules and Representations.* New York: Columbia University Press.

Chomsky, Noam. 1980b. "On Cognitive Structures and Their Development: A Reply to Piaget." In Piattelli-Palmarini, Massimo (Ed.). 1980. *Language and Learning: The debate between Jean Piaget and Noam Chomsky*, 35-54. Cambridge, MA: Harvard University Press.

Chomsky, Noam. 1981. *Lectures on government and binding.* Dordrecht: Foris.

Chomsky, Noam. 1995. *The Minimalist Program.* Cambridge, MA: The MIT Press.

Clark, Alexander. 2001. *Unsupervised Language Acquisition: Theory and Practice.* Ph.D. Dissertation, University of Sussex.

Clark, Eve. 1971. "On the acquisition of the meaning of "before" and "after"," *Journal of Verbal Learning and Verbal Behavior*, 10, 266-275.

Conway, Laura, and Stephen Crain. 1995. "Dynamic Acquisition." In *Proceedings of the 19th Boston University Conference on Language Development*, 180-191. Somerville, MA: Cascadilla Press.

Crain, Stephen. 1982 "Temporal terms: Mastery by age five," *Papers and Reports on Child Language Development*, 21, 33-38.

Crain, Stephen. 1991. "Language acquisition in the absence of experience," *Behavioral and Brain Sciences*, 597-650.

Crain, Stephen, Andrea Gualmini and Luisa Meroni. 2000. "The Acquisition of Logical Words," *Logos and Language*, 1, 49-59.

Crain, Stephen. 2002. "Sense and sense ability in child language." In *Proceedings of the 24th Boston University Conference on Language Development*, 22-44. Somerville, MA: Cascadilla Press.

Crain, Stephen, and Cecile McKee. 1985. "The acquisition of structural restrictions on anaphora." In *Proceedings of NELS 15*, 94-110. Amherst, MA: GLSA.

Crain, Stephen, and Mark Steedman. 1985. "On not being led up the garden path: The use of context by the psychological parser." In David Dowty, Lauri Karttunen and Arnold Zwicky (Eds.) *Natural Language Parsing: Psychological, Computational and Theoretical Perspectives*, 320-354. Cambridge: Cambridge University Press.

Crain, Stephen, and Mineharu Nakayama. 1987. "Structure dependence in grammar formation," *Language*, 63, 522-543.

Crain, Stephen, Weijia Ni and Laura Conway. 1994. "Learning, parsing and modularity." In Charles Clifton, Lyn Frazier and Keith Rayner (Eds.) *Perspectives on sentence processing*, 443-467. Hillsdale, NJ: LEA.

Crain, Stephen, Rosalind Thornton, Carol Boster, Laura Conway, Diane Lillo-Martin and Elaine Woodams. 1996. "Quantification without qualification," *Language Acquisition*, 5, 83-153.

Crain, Stephen, and Rosalind Thornton. 1998. *Investigations in Universal Grammar*. Cambridge, MA: The MIT Press.

Crain, Stephen, and Ken Wexler. 1999. "Methodology in the study of language acquisition: A modular approach." In William C. Ritchie and Tej K. Bhatia (Eds.) *Handbook of Language Acquisition*, 387-425. San Diego: Academic Press.

Crain, Stephen, and Paul Pietroski. 2001. "Nature, Nurture and Universal Grammar," *Linguistics and Philosophy*, 24, 139-186.

Crain, Stephen, Amanda Gardner, Andrea Gualmini and Beth Rabbin. 2002. "Children's Command of Negation." In *Proceedings of the Third Tokyo Conference on Psycholinguistics*, 71-95, Tokyo: Hituzi Publishing Company.

Crain, Stephen, and Paul Pietroski. 2002. "Why language acquisition is a 'snap'," *The Linguistic Review*, 19, 163-183.

Crain, Stephen, Andrea Gualmini and Paul Pietroski, 2003. "Brass Tacks in Linguistic Theory" To appear in *Proceedings of the First Annual AHRB Conference on Innateness and the Structure of the Mind*.

De Villiers, Jill, and Helen Tager Flusberg. 1975. "Some facts one simply cannot deny," *Journal of Child Language*, 2, 279-286.

De Swart, Henriette, and Ivan Sag. 2002. "Negation and Negative Concord in Romance," *Linguistics and Philosophy*, 25, 373-417.

Diesing, Molly. 1992. *Indefinites*. Cambridge, MA: The MIT Press.

Donaldson, M. and P. Lloyd. 1974: "Sentences and situations: Children's judgments of match and mismatch." In F. Bresson (Ed.), *Problèmes Actuels en Psycholinguistique*. Paris: Centre National de la Recherche Scientifique.

Drozd, Kenneth. 2000. "Children's weak interpretation of universally quantified sentences." In Melissa Bowerman and Stephen Levinson (Eds.) *Conceptual Development and Language Acquisition*, 340-376. Cambridge: Cambridge University Press.

Drozd, Kenneth, and Erik van Loosbroek. 1998. "Weak quantification, plausible dissent, and the development of children's pragmatic competence." In *Proceedings of the 23rd Boston University Conference on Language Development,* 184-195. Somerville, MA: Cascadilla Press.

Drozd, Kenneth, and Erik van Loosbroek. 1999. *The effect of context on children's interpretation of universally quantified sentences.* Ms., Max Planck Institute for Psycholinguistics and Nijmegen University, Nijmegen.

Elman, Jeffrey. 1990. "Finding structure in time," *Cognitive Science,* 14, 179-211.

Farkas, Donka. 2002. "Varieties of Indefinites." In *Proceedings of Semantic and Linguistic Theory (SALT) XII.* Ithaca, NY: CLC Publications.

von Fintel, Kai. 1994. *Restrictions on Quantifiers Domain.* Ph.D. Dissertation, University of Massachusetts at Amherst.

von Fintel, Kai. 1999. "NPI-licensing, Strawson-entailment, and context-dependency," *Journal of Semantics,* 16, 97-148.

Fodor, Janet, and Stephen Crain. 1987. "Simplicity and generality of rules in language acquisition." In Brian MacWhinney (Ed.) *Mechanisms of language acquisition.* Hillsdale, NJ: Erlbaum.

Fodor, Janet, and Carrie Crowther. 2002. "Understanding stimulus poverty arguments," *The Linguistic Review,* 19, 105-145.

Fox, Danny. 2002. "Antecedent-Contained Deletion and the Copy Theory of Movement," *Linguistic Inquiry,* 33, 63-96.

Freeman, Norman H., C.G. Sinha and Jacqueline A. Stedmon. 1982. "All the cars –which cars? From word to meaning to discourse analysis." In Michael Beveridge (Ed.) *Children thinking through language,* 52-74. London: Edward Arnold Publisher.

Freeman, Norman H., and Jacqueline A. Stedmon. 1986. "How children deal with natural language quantification." In Ida Kurcz, Grace Wales Shugar and Joseph H. Danks (Eds.) *Knowledge and Language,* 21-48. Amsterdam: Elesevier Science Publishers.

Geurts, Bart. 2000. "Book Review. Stephen Crain and Rosalind Thornton. Investigations in Universal Grammar: A Guide to Experiments on the Acquisition of Syntax and Semantics," *Linguistics and Philosophy,* 23 (5), 523-532

Geurts, Bart. 2001. *Quantifying Kinds.* Ms., Humboldt University, Berlin and Nijmegen University, Nijmegen.

Giannakidou, Anastasia. 1997. *The Landscape of Polarity Items.* Ph.D. Dissertation, University of Groningen.

Giannakidou, Anastasia. 1998. *Polarity Sensitivity and (Non)veridical Dependency*. Amsterdam: John Benjamins.

Givon, Talmy. 1978. "Negation in Language: Pragmatics, Function, Ontology." In Peter Cole (Ed.) *Syntax and Semantics 9: Pragmatics*, 69-112. New York: Academic Press.

Glenberg, Arthus, David Robertson, Jennifer Jansen and Mina Johnsonn-Glenberg. 1999. "Not propositions," *Journal of Cognitive Systems Research*, 1, 19-33.

Gordon, Peter. 1996. "The Truth Value Judgment Task." In Dana McDaniel, Cecile McKee and Helen Smith Cairns (Eds.) *Methods for Assessing Children's Syntax*, 211-231. Cambridge, Mass: The MIT Press.

Gouro, Takuya, Hanae Norita, Motoki Nakajima and Ken-ichi Ariji. 2001. "Children's Interpretation of Universal Quantifier and Pragmatic Interference." In *Proceedings of the Second Tokyo University Conference on Psycholinguistics*, 61-78. Tokyo: Hituzi Publishing Company.

Grice, Paul. 1975. "Logic and Conversation," in Peter Cole and James Morgan (Eds.) *Syntax and Semantics 3; Speech Acts*. New York: Academic Press. Reprinted in *Studies on the Way of Words*, 22-57. Cambridge, Massachusetts: Harvard university Press.

Grimshaw, Jane, and Sara T. Rosen. 1990. "Knowledge and Obedience. The developmental status of the binding theory," *Linguistic Inquiry*, 21, 187-222.

Gualmini, Andrea. 2001. "The Unbearable Lightness of Scalar Implicatures." Doctoral Research Paper, University of Maryland at College Park.

Gualmini, Andrea, Stephen Crain, Luisa Mero, Gennaro Chierchia and Maria Teresa Guasti. 2001. "At the Semantics/Pragmatics Interface in Child Language." In *Proceedings of Semantics and Linguistic Theory (SALT) 11*, 231-247. Ithaca, NY: Cornell University.

Gualmini, Andrea, Luisa Meroni and Stephen Crain. 2003. "An Asymmetric Universal in Child Language." In *Proceedings of Sinn und Bedeutung VII*, 136-148.

Konstanz: Konstanz Linguistics Working Papers.

Guasti, Maria Teresa. 1994. "Verb syntax in Italian child grammar: finite and non-finite verbs," *Language Acquisition, 3*, 1-40.

Grinstead, John. 1994. *Consequences of the maturation of number morphology in Spanish and Catalan*. Unpublished MA Thesis, University of California at Los Angeles.

Heim, Irene. 1982. *The Semantics of Definite and Indefinite Noun Phrases.* Ph.D. Dissertation, University of Massachusetts, Amherst.

Higginbotham, James. 1991. "Either/or," in *Proceedings of NELS 21*, 143-155. Amherst, MA: GLSA.

Hoecksema, Jacob. 1999. "Blocking Effects and Polarity Sensitivity." In Jelle Gerbrandy, Maarten Marx, Maarten de Rijke and Yde Venema (Eds.) *JFAK. Essays dedicated to Johan van Benthem on the Occasion of his 50th Birthday.* Amsterdam: Amsterdam University Press.

Hoecksema, Jacob. 2000. "Negative Polarity Items: Triggering, Scope and C-Command." In Laurence Horn and Yasuhiko Kato (Eds.) *Negation and Polarity. Semantic and Syntactic Perspectives*, 123-154. Oxford: Oxford University Press.

Hoekstra, Teun, and Nina Hyams. 1998. "Aspects of root infinitives," *Lingua*, 106, 81-112.

Horn, Laurence. 1989. *A Natural History of Negation.* Chicago: University of Chicago Press.

Hurewitz, Felicia, Lila Gleitman and Rochel Gelman. 2002. "On the acquisition of numbers and quantifiers: *some, all, two* and *four* at three." Paper presented at *The 27th Annual Boston University Conference on Language Development*, November 1-3, 2002, Boston, MA.

Inhelder, Barbel, and Jean Piaget. 1964. *The early growth of logic in the child.* London: Routledge, Kegan and Paul.

Israel, Michael. 1998. *The Rhetoric of Grammar: Scalar reasoning and Polarity Sensitivity.* Ph.D. Dissertation, University of California, San Diego.

Jespersen, Otto. 1909-1949. *A Modern English Grammar on Historical Principles.* London: George, Allen and Unwin Ltd..

Kurtzman, Howard, and Maryellen MacDonald. 1993. "Resolution of Quantifier Scope Ambiguities," *Cognition*, 48, 243-279

Kadmon, Nirit, and Fred Landman, 1993. "Any," *Linguistics and Philosophy*, 16, 353-422.

Kamp, Hans. 1981. "A theory of truth and semantic interpretation." In Jeroen Groenendijk, Theo Janssen, and Martin Stokhof (Eds.), *Formal Methods in the Study of Language*, 277-322. Amsterdam: Mathematical Centre.

Kamp, Hans, and Uwe Ryle. 1993. *From Discourse to Logic.* Dordrecht: Kluwer.

Keenan, Edward L. and Jonathan Stavi. 1986. "A semantic characterization of natural language determiners," *Linguistics and Philosophy*, 9, 253-326.

Klima, Edward S. 1964. "Negation in English." In Jerry A. Fodor and Jerrold J. Katz (Eds.) *The structure of language*. Englewood Cliffs: Prentice Hall.

Koster, Charlotte, and Sjoukje van der Wal. 1995. "Acquiring a negative polarity verb." In *Papers from the Dutch-German colloquium on language acquisition*, 92-102. Amsterdam: Amsterdam Series in Child Language Development.

Krämer, Irene. 2000. *Interpreting Indefinites. An Experimental Study of Children's Language comprehension*. Ph.D. Dissertation, MPI Series. Wageningen: Ponsen & Looijen.

Kratzer, Angelika. 1995. "Stage-level and individual-level predicates as inherent generics." In Gregory Carlson and Francis Jeffrey Pelletier (Eds.) *The Generic Book*, 125-175. Chicago: University of Chicago Press.

Krifka, Manfred. 1995. "The semantics and pragmatics and polarity items," *Linguistic Analysis*, 25, 209-257.

Lasnik, Howard, and Juan Uriagereka. 2002. "On the poverty of the challenge," *The Linguistic Review*, 19, 147-150.

Ladusaw, William. 1979. *Negative Polarity Items as Inherent Scope Relations*. Ph.D. Dissertation, University of Texas at Austin.

Ladusaw, William. 1980. *Negative Polarity Items as Inherent Scope Relations*. New York: Garland.

Ladusaw, William. 1992. "Expressing Negation." In *Proceedings of Semantics and Linguistic Theory (SALT) II*, 237-259.

Levinson, Stephen. 2000. *Presumptive Meanings*. Cambridge, MA: The MIT Press.

Lewis, David. 1975. "Adverbs of Quantification." In Edward Keenan (Ed.) *Formal Semantics of Natural Language*, 3-15. Cambridge: Cambridge University Press.

Lewis, David. 1979. "Scorekeeping in a language game," *Journal of Philosophical Logic*, 8, 339-359.

Lewis, John, and Jeffrey Elman. 2002. "Learnability and the statistical structure of language: Poverty of stimulus arguments revisited." In *Proceedings of the 26th Annual Boston University Conference on Language Development*, 359-370. Somerville, MA: Cascadilla Press.

Lidz, Jeffrey, and Julien Musolino. 2002. "Children's command of quantification," *Cognition*, 84, 113-154.

Linebarger, Marcia. 1980. *The Grammar of Negative Polarity*. Ph.D. Dissertation, Massachusetts Institute of Technology, Cambridge, MA.

Linebarger, Marcia 1987. "Negative Polarity and Grammatical Representation," *Linguistics and Philosophy*, 10, 325-387.

Ludlow, Peter. 2002. "LF and Natural Logic." In Gerhard Preyer (Ed.) *Logical Form, Language and Ontology: On Contemporary Developments in the Philosophy of Language and Linguistics*. Oxford: Oxford University Press.

MacNamara, John. 1982. *Names for Things*. Cambridge, MA: The MIT Press.

Matthewson, Lisa. 1999. "On the Interpretation of Wide-Scope Indefinites," *Natural Language Semantics*, 7, 79-134.

May, Robert. 1977. *The Grammar of Quantification*. Ph.D. Dissertation, Massachusetts Institute of Technology, Cambridge, MA.

May, Robert. 1989. "Interpreting Logical Form," *Linguistics and Philosophy*, 12, 387-435.

McDaniel, Dana, and Helen Smith Cairns. 1996. "Eliciting Judgments of Grammaticality and Reference," In Dana McDaniel, Cecile McKee and Helen Smith Cairns (Eds.) *Methods for Assessing Children's Syntax*, 233-254. Cambridge, MA: The MIT Press.

Meroni, Luisa. 2002. "Children's and adults' interpretation of the universal quantifier: Grammatical non-adult principles vs. non-grammatical adult principles." Doctoral Research Paper, University of Maryland at College Park.

Meroni, Luisa, Andrea Gualmini and Stephen Crain. 2000. "A conservative approach to quantification in child language." In *Proceedings of the 24th Annual Penn Linguistics Colloquium*, 171-182. Philadelphia, PA: UPenn.

Meroni, Luisa, Andrea Gualmini and Stephen Crain. 2001. "Three Years of Continuous Acquisition," In *Proceedings of the Second Tokyo Conference on Psycholinguistics*, 1-33. Tokyo: Hituzi Publishing Company.

Meroni, Luisa, Andrea Gualmini and Stephen Crain. 2003. "Everybody knows." Ms., University of Maryland.

Milsark, Gary. 1974. *Existential Sentences in English*, Ph.D. Dissertation, Massachusetts Institute of Technology, Cambridge, MA.

Milsark, Gary. 1977. "Toward an explanation of certain peculiarities of the existential construction in English," *Linguistic Analysis*, 3, 1-29.

Musolino, Julien. 1998. *Universal Grammar and the Acquisition of Semantic Knowledge: an Experimental Investigation into the Acquisition of Quantifier-Negation Interaction in English*. Ph.D. Dissertation, University of Maryland at College Park.

Musolino, Julien. 2001. "Structure and Meaning in the Acquisition of Scope." Ms. Indiana University.

Musolino, Julien, Stephen Crain and Rosalind Thornton. 2000. "Navigating negative quantificational space," *Linguistics*, 38, 1-32.

Musolino, Julien, and Jeffrey Lidz. 2002a. "Preschool Logic: Truth and Felicity in the Acquisition of Quantification." In *Proceedings of the 26th Boston University Conference on Language Development*, 406-416. Somerville, MA: Cascadilla Press.

Musolino, Julien, and Jeffrey Lidz. 2002b. "Why children aren't universally successful with quantification." Ms., Indiana University and Northwestern University.

Nakayama, Mineharu. 1987. "Performance factors in subject-auxiliary inversion," *Journal of Child Language*, 14, 113-126

O'Leary, Carrie, and Stephen Crain. 1994. "Negative Polarity Items (a Positive Result) and Positive Polarity Items (a Negative Result)." Paper presented at the *19th Boston University Conference on Language Development*. Boston, MA.

Partee, Barbara, Alice ter Meulen and Robert Wall. 1990. *Mathematical Methods in Linguistics*. Dordrecht: Kluwer.

Philip, William. 1995. *Event quantification in the acquisition of universal quantification*. Ph.D. Dissertation, University of Massachusetts, Amherst, MA.

Philip, William. 1996. "The Event Quantificational Account of Symmetrical Interpretation and a Denial of Implausible Infelicity." In *Proceedings of the 20th Boston University Conference on Language Development*, 564-575. Somerville, MA: Cascadilla Press.

Philip, William, and Emily Lynch. 2000. "Felicity, Relevance, and Acquisition of the Grammar of *Every* and *Only*." In *Proceedings of the 24th Boston University Conference on Language Development*, 583-596. Somerville, MA: Cascadilla Press.

Piattelli-Palmarini, Massimo (Ed.). 1980. *Language and Learning: The debate between Jean Piaget and Noam Chomsky*. Cambridge, MA: Harvard University Press.

Pinker, Steven. 1984. *Language learnability and language development*. Cambridge, MA: Harvard University Press.

Poeppel, David, and Ken Wexler. 1993. "The full competence hypothesis of clause structure in early German," *Language*, 69, 1-33.

Postal, Paul. 1971. *Cross-over Phenomena*. New York: Holt, Rinehart & Winston.

Potts, Christopher. 2000. "When even *no*'s neg is splitsville." Contribution to *Jorge Hankamer's Web Fest*. At http://ling.ucsc.edu//Jorge/index.html.

Potts, Christopher. 2001. "The syntax and semantics of *As*-parentheticals," *Natural Language and Linguistic Theory*, 20, 623-689.

Progovac, Ljiljana. 1988. *A binding approach to polarity sensitivity.* Ph.D. Dissertation. University of Southern California, Los Angeles.

Progovac, Ljiljana. 1994. *Negative and positive polarity. A binding approach.* Cambridge: Cambridge University Press.

Pullum, Geoffrey, and Barbara Scholz. 2002. "Empirical Assessment of the stimulus poverty argument," *The Linguistic Review*, 19, 9-50.

Reinhart, Tanya. 1976. *The Syntactic Domain of Anaphora.* Ph.D. dissertation, Massachusetts Institute of Technology, Cambridge, MA.

Reinhart, Tanya. 1995. *Interface Strategies.* Utrecht: OTS working papers in linguistics.

Reinhart, Tanya. 1997. "Quantifier Scope: how labor is divided between QR and choice functions," *Linguistics and Philosophy*, 20, 335-397.

Rizzi, Luigi. 1994. "Some Notes on Linguistic Theory and Language Development," *Language Acquisition,* 3, 371-393.

Roeper, Tom, and Jill de Villiers. 1991. "The Emergence of Bound Variable Structures." In T. Maxfield and Plunket (Eds.) *University of Massachusetts Occasional Papers: Papers in the Acquisition of WH,* 267-282. Amherts, MA: GLSA.

Rosenbaum, Peter. 1967. *The Grammar of English Predicate Constructions.* Cambridge, MA: The MIT Press.

Russell, Bertrand. 1948. *Human knowledge: Its scope and limits.* London: Allen.

Sampson, Geoffrey. 1999. *Educating Eve.* London: Cassell.

Sampson, Geoffrey. 2002. "Exploring the richness of the stimulus," *The Linguistic Review*, 19, 73-104.

Savarese, Fred. 1999. *Studies in Coreference and Binding.* Ph.D. Dissertation, University of Maryland at College Park.

Scholz, Barbara, and Geoffrey Pullum. 2002. "Searching for arguments to support linguistic nativism," *The Linguistic Review*, 19, 185-223.

Smith, Linda B. 1999. "Children's noun learning: How general processes make specialized learning mechanisms." In Brian MacWhinney (Ed.) *The emergence of language.* Mahwah, NJ: LEA

Sugisaki, Koji, and Miwa Isobe. 2001. "Quantification without Qualification without Plausible Dissent." *University of Massachusetts Occasional Papers in Linguistics*, 25, 97-100. Amherst, MA: GLSA.

Szabolcsi, Anna. 2002a. "Positive Polarity – Negative Polarity." To appear in *Natural Language and Linguistic Theory.*

Szabolcsi, Anna. 2002b. "Hungarian disjunctions and positive polarity." In I. Kenesei and P. Siptár (Eds.) *Approaches to Hungarian 8*, 217-241. Budapest: Akadémiai Kiadó.

Thornton, Rosalind. 1990. *Adventure in long-distance moving: The acquisition of complex wh-questions*. Ph.D. dissertation, University of Connecticut, Storrs.

Thornton. Rosalind. 1994. "Children's Negative Questions: A Production/Comprehension Asymmetry." In *Proceedings of ESCOL*, 306-317. Ithaca, NY: Cornell University.

Thornton, Rosalind. 1996. "Elicited Production." In Dana McDaniel, Cecile McKee and Helen Smith Cairns (Eds.) *Methods for Assessing Children's Syntax*, 77-102. Cambridge, MA: The MIT Press.

Thornton, Rosalind, and Ken Wexler. 1999. *Principle B, VP Ellipsis, and Interpretation in Child Grammar*. Cambridge, MA: The MIT Press.

Tomasello, Michael. 2000. "Do young children have adult syntactic competence?", *Cognition*, 70, 209-253.

van Benthem, Johan. 1984. "Questions about quantifiers," *Journal of Symbolic Logic*, 49, 443-466.

van Geenhoven, Veerle. 1998. *Semantic Incorporation and indefinite descriptions: Semantic and syntactic aspects of noun incorporation in West Greenlandic*. Stanford, CA: CSLI Publications.

van der Wal, Sjoukje. 1996. *Negative Polarity Items and Negation, Tandem Acquisition*. Groningen: Groningen Dissertation in Linguistics.

van der Wouden, Ton. 1994. *Negative contexts*. Ph.D. Dissertation. University of Groningen.

Wason, Peter. 1965. "The context of plausible denial," *Journal of Verbal Learning and Verbal Behaviour*, 4, 7-11.

Wason, Peter. 1972. "In Real Life Negatives Are False," *Logique et Analyse*, 15, 17-38.

Waxman, Sandra R. 2002. "Early word learning and conceptual development: Everything had a name, and each name gave birth to a new thought." In Usha Goswami (Ed.) *Blackwell Handbook of Childhood Cognitive Development*, 102-126. Oxford, UK: Blackwell Publishers.

Westerståhl, Dag. 1985. "Logical constants in quantifier languages," *Linguistics and Philosophy*, 8, 387-413.

Wexler, Ken. 2002. "Lenneberg's Dream: Learning Normal Language Development and Specific Language Impairment," in J. Schaffer and Y. Levy (Eds.) *Language Competence Across Populations: Towards a Definition of Specific Language Impairment*. Mahwah, NJ: Erlbaum.

Wexler, Ken. 1994. "Optional infinitives, verb movement and the economy of derivation in child grammar." In David Lightfoot and Norbert Hornstein (Eds.) *Verb Movement*, 305-382. Cambridge: Cambridge University Press.

Winter, Yoad. 1997. "Choice Functions and the Scopal Semantics of Indefinites," *Linguistics and Philosophy*, 20, 399-467

Zwarts, Frans. 1998. "Three Types of Polarity." In Fritz Hamm and Erhard Hinrichs (Eds.) *Plurality and Quantification*, 177-238. Dordrecht: Kluwer.

Index of Names

Index of Topics

For Product Safety Concerns and Information please contact our EU
representative GPSR@taylorandfrancis.com Taylor & Francis Verlag GmbH,
Kaufingerstraße 24, 80331 München, Germany

Printed and bound by CPI Group (UK) Ltd, Croydon, CR0 4YY
08/06/2025
01897001-0012